faith
forward

rené schlaepfer

Interior and cover design: 7Roots Creative

Want to see sermons, small group videos, and more related to this book?

www.tlc.org/faithforward

introduction   5

daily devotions   10-176

small group lessons

endnotes   .   211

intro-
duction

If fear is cultivated it will become stronger.
If faith is cultivated it will achieve mastery.
– John Paul Jones

Your faith is thin.
You really tried.
But now you're tapped out.
Demoralized.
Done.

Relationship stress, church division, and most of all, a long period of national and international anxiety have you feeling traumatized and exhausted. Faith that was once a source of strength is now in need of a recharge. Simply put: you're tired of waiting for things to get better.

Would it surprise you to learn that a book in the Bible was written to people feeling exactly the same way?

The Book of Hebrews was meant for first-century believers in Jesus who started with a lot of enthusiasm, but were now so tired. Tired of persecution. Tired of politics. Tired of waiting for God to set things right.

They'd been worshipping enthusiastically and giving generously because they thought of themselves as ambassadors of the coming kingdom.

But it is *taking… so… long…* Things just seem to be getting worse. Many are slipping from the fellowship. Discouraged. Disillusioned. Divided.

Then, in one of the most beautiful, poetic, surprising, epic chapters of the Bible, the author of the Book of Hebrews introduces a parade of people who kept the faith.

The eleventh chapter of Hebrews is known as the Hall of Fame of Faith. These walls are lined with portraits of quirky characters: An 80-year-old shepherd who took on a king; a prostitute who collaborated with spies; a cowardly warrior who led a nation. It's full of exciting scenes: Menacing Pharaohs and crumbling fortresses and wild animals and heavenly cities. I'd like to be your tour guide. Let's walk through these scenes and linger on these portraits to discover their weird and wonderful stories.

Here's my favorite part. Hebrews 11 has a surprise ending. I promise. If you hang in there, I guarantee there will be a twist at the end that — well, it gives me goose bumps, anyway.

Come with me. Your faith will grow richer. Your optimism will soar higher. Your confidence will be stronger.

First, a little introduction to this fascinating part of the Bible–

and why it's so relevant for us today.

———————————

The Book of Hebrews is a bit of a mystery. It reads like a fragment of a very ancient letter by an anonymous author to a group of unknown believers. That's because it's a fragment of a very ancient letter by an anonymous author to a group of unknown believers. We don't really know who it was written to, but we know what they were struggling with because of the issues addressed by the author: They were demoralized, discouraged, and doubtful.

We also don't know who wrote it. Lots of names have been suggested. Paul. Barnabas. Apollos. Priscilla. Even in the first century there was no consensus on its authorship. Around 200 A.D., Origen said, "Who wrote the epistle is known to God alone." But Christians loved it because it's beautiful. Even secular scholars consider it a masterpiece of Greek writing.

I like that it's a mystery. Because it makes it easier to imagine it's written straight to you and me. Sure fits where we're at right now.

So many intense things have happened.
A global pandemic.
Social upheaval.
Political division.
The rise of weird anti-Christian sentiment.
The rise of weird Christians.

When the first wave of all this trouble hit, many of us were creative and resilient. We volunteered, we did church virtually, we took remote classes, we donated to good causes. We reached out to neighbors. We looked for silver linings.

But now?

Exhaustion, confusion, division—all up.
Volunteerism, church attendance, charitable giving—all down.

Here's why that's bad: Those are the very best ways our resilience is actually increased. Experts have done research on soldiers returning from war to find out why some seem to handle the post-traumatic stress better than others. What makes some more resilient? They tend to have these three things in their lives:

- **Community**: a support group
- **Generosity**: volunteering or serving
- **Theology:** a faith-based world view that God is ultimately in control.

But there's a problem. When we are traumatized, we start to withdraw from those very things. That's exactly what was happening to the original readers of Hebrews. So the author encourages them,

> "And let us consider how we may **spur one another on** toward love and good deeds, **not giving up meeting together**, as some are in the habit of doing, but **encouraging one another**—and all the more as you see the Day approaching." (Hebrews 10:24-25)

As we start this journey together, that's great direction for us too. So find some friends to study with. Read Hebrews 11.

Then we'll go through it one section at a time in these pages.

This is not just about you and your sense of optimism. There are people all around you ready to give up. Your family, community, and church need you to be a person of courageous faith, someone who sees beyond the often overwhelming headlines and trusts that God is ultimately in control, someone who speaks words of encouragement to those ready to quit, someone who is totally honest about their struggles yet also believes there is a great future ahead, someone who knows that what we do now really does make a difference, someone who takes one step at a time through the darkness believing there is light ahead.

There are enough naysayers and doomcasters, enough cynics and critics. Let's get intentionally recentered on what motivated these oppressed, depressed, and hard-pressed people in Hebrews 11 to stand up and stand out, to be confident and courageous, to keep walking and keep believing.

Let's learn to live faith forward!

1
crisis of faith

**Do not throw away
your confidence; it
will be richly rewarded.**

(Hebrews 10:35)

The stress many of us feel is really a lack of faith.
– Francis Chan

My wife Laurie is in line at the post office the other day and overhears the woman in front of her proclaiming to the clerk at the window, "Every time I turn on the news, it's a disaster!" The clerk responds, "A disaster! A disaster! And I just heard there's gonna be solar flares this week that will ruin cell service!"

And then this clerk turns to the man working next to her and says, "Oh I'm sorry, we're probably depressing you."

And he says, in a voice loud enough to be heard throughout the building, "NOT ANY MORE DEPRESSED THAN I ALREADY AM. I'M SO DEPRESSED ALREADY I COULD NOT GO ANY LOWER. I AM AS LOW AS LOW CAN GO."

Just as Laurie thinks, "I'm going to invite them to church!" the first clerk asks the second, "What does the Bible say about all this?"

And before my wife can say a word, he answers, "THE **BIBLE**? HEY, THE **CHRISTIANS** ARE EVEN WORSE THAN US!" Sort of like, in the self-evaluation of postal workers, they know they're not known for being the most optimistic people on earth—but Christians? They're even worse!

You know what? Some of us deserve that. Many Christians are stuck in a negative mindset. I suspect there are two reasons.

First, we're exposed to bad news constantly. Talk show hosts, headline apps, bloggers, cable news, and all the other voices in the news ecosystem are fighting to be heard. Research tells them the best way to get views and clicks and likes is to go negative. So they do. With growing expertise.

Second, we have lived through a genuinely alarming time. Most of us did pretty well in the early months of the upheaval that swept the world in 2020. Now many of us are showing signs of being stress-saturated, grief-stricken, and traumatized. We are on edge.

We relate to that clerk:
"I AM AS LOW AS LOW CAN GO."

That's the situation the first readers of Hebrews found themselves in. Look how the author reminds them of their previously positive attitude:

> "Remember those earlier days after you had received the light, when you endured in a great conflict full of suffering. Sometimes you were publicly exposed to insult and persecution; at other times you stood side by side with those who were mistreated. You suffered along with those in prison…" (Hebrews 10:32-34a)

Right. But now they're done. Fatigued. Disillusioned.
They sacrificed and persevered and fought the good fight.
But for what?
The goal posts keep moving.
The situation is not improving.
Their team is down by a million points.
Their frustration is feeding a spirit of criticism.
Sound familiar?

So their coach encourages them:

> "Do not throw away your confidence; it will be richly rewarded." (Hebrews 10:35)

That's the root problem. Not their circumstances. Their confidence. Without confidence that things will improve, hopelessness sets in. Without hope, decay and despair take over.

The downward spiral must be stopped.

Much was at stake for these early believers. To "throw away your confidence" meant not just giving in to cynicism. It meant abandoning the Jesus project. They had really believed the vision of the kingdom taught by Jesus: a new community characterized by love for God and for each other that would one day be fully manifested in the new heaven and new earth when Jesus returned.

Ok, but. Decades after buying into all that, these first Christians are looking around, seeing the world get worse and the church get stale. They are losing faith.

There's hope, though. By saying, "don't throw away your confidence," the author must mean they still have a vestige of confidence. A weak heartbeat. A spark. Their faith is not dead yet. So, the writer says, let's breathe life into it.

Could your own faith use some spiritual CPR?
Want to return to that hope you once felt?

This is the way forward.

2
faith to
persevere

You need to persevere...

(Hebrews 10:36a)

**The principle part of faith is patience.
– George Mueller**

"Are we there yet?" has to be the most frequently asked question we heard when driving our three kids to Disneyland one summer. Every. Ten. Minutes. To a little kid, a 300-mile road trip may as well be a trip to the moon. It is incomprehensible. When they climbed into their car seats our children expected to see the peak of the Matterhorn almost instantly. After all, that's the destination we promised. Instead they saw the mind-numbing monotony of Interstate 5. We kept reassuring them, "We are getting closer! We have a plan!" I think they started to lose faith in us many times.

To try and silence that question just a little bit, my wife Laurie made a road map featuring drawings of the iconic sights they would see along the way. The McDonald's playland we would reach halfway. The roller coasters of Magic Mountain. The lake at the top of the Grapevine pass. Each of our kids got a map so they could be reassured that Mom and Dad really were not just driving aimlessly. There is a destination. Every mile we're a mile closer.

That's sort of what the author of Hebrews does to help these discouraged believers. Here's how he sets up his purpose for chapter 11:

> "You need to persevere, so that when you have done the will of God, you will receive what he has promised. For, 'In just a little while, he who is coming will come and will not delay.'" (Hebrews 10:36-37)

That last line is a paraphrase from the Old Testament book

Habakkuk. It starts with Habakkuk complaining to God. He's tired. He doesn't like the way things are. He wants God to do something. He is asking, "Why are we not there yet?!" This quote is God's reassurance that a new day is coming.

What follows in Hebrews 11 is like that illustrated road map for our kids, featuring vivid portraits of iconic Bible heroes on their own road to faith. It's as if the writer is saying, "See? Others have travelled this path before you. Hang in there. We're getting closer."

But first… back to Habakkuk (say that five times fast). Here's what living by faith looks like when the view outside your window is the featureless 5 instead of the spires of Space Mountain. Habakkuk wraps up his book like this:

> "Though the fig tree does not bud
> and there are no grapes on the vines,
> though the olive crop fails
> and the fields produce no food,
> though there are no sheep in the pen
> and no cattle in the stalls,
> yet I will rejoice in the Lord,
> I will be joyful in God my Savior.
> The Sovereign Lord is my strength;
> he makes my feet like the feet of a deer,
> he enables me to tread on the heights."
> (Habakkuk 3:17-19)

How do you get to that place of faith in spite of dire circumstances? Let's dive into one of the most famous chapters in the whole Bible.

3
how faith thinks

Now faith is confidence in what we hope for
and assurance about what we do not see.
This is what the ancients were commended for.

(Hebrews 11:1,2)

Faith has hope past the horizon.

What is faith?

Hard question. It's like asking, "what is blue?" How would you answer that? You'd probably point to things that are blue.

The sky is blue.
That bird is blue.
The ocean is blue.
Look at them and you'll understand.

That's kind of what the author does in Hebrews 11.

That guy had faith.
That woman had faith.
Those people had faith.
Look at their stories and you'll start to figure it out.

But before the author gets into their stories, these early verses of Hebrews 11 have some brilliant and inspiring observations about faith.

First, faith is "confidence in what we hope for and assurance about what we do not see." (Hebrews 11:1)

> "Faith is taking the first step even when you don't see the whole staircase." – Martin Luther King, Jr.

Faith moves. Faith acts. Faith advances with hope beyond the horizon. When you think about it, this is essential to progress in any field.

In 1960, when President Kennedy said, "Before the end of this decade, we will put a man on the moon," the technology to do that had not even been invented.

Take the church I serve, Twin Lakes Church in Santa Cruz. In 1973 Roy Kraft and Glen Ifland envisioned the entire campus long before one building was built. As I write this, we are opening a college center exactly where they saw one when there was only dirt.

In 2013 when we proposed to the church that we build a children's education building, a college ministry building, and a medical clinic in India, and that we support our local food bank with one million meals, that was all just a paragraph on a piece of paper. Now it is all reality.

To do *anything* you need to be confident of what you do not see.

To clarify: Biblical faith is not just positive thinking. Now, positive thinking is good. As Rick Warren says, "What's the alternative? Negative thinking? But positive thinking is limited. If you're in the middle of a snowstorm in your pajamas you could have tons of positive thinking, but you'd still be freezing." And faith is definitely not saying, "Everything will go just the way I plan." Because almost nothing in life goes the way you plan!

Faith is the confident assurance that God is in control of the future. He is driving. We are getting somewhere. So I can keep going.

Then the author of Hebrews says, "This is what the ancients

were commended for." (Hebrews 11:2)

The ancients. OK, this is super-important.

The readers of Hebrews are being reassured that this idea of salvation by faith is not something new. This is the way God has always operated.

Way before Christianity, before Judaism, in the days of the "ancients", the way to God was always through faith.

The author of Hebrews is about to prove it.

So faith is moving forward with hope in the dark. But that's not the only component of faith. If you stopped there it could just be sheer grit or even foolish presumption. There are two other crucial facets of living faith forward.

4
faith is entrustment

And without faith it is impossible to please God, because anyone who approaches Him must believe that He exists and that He rewards those who earnestly seek Him.

(Hebrews 11:6)

**Faith is not just something I think.
Faith is something I live.**

When my mother Rosemarie was in her seventies, Alzheimer's disease began robbing her of the ability to think clearly. Even speech became difficult. Before it distanced her from me completely, I wanted to know her answer to a puzzle I had been pondering for quite some time.

"Mom," I asked, "You have been through so many losses. You lived on the border of Germany all through World War Two. You were widowed twice. You experienced poverty as a single parent of two toddlers. You lost many of your belongings in a fire. Now Alzheimer's. Yet you have always seemed confident and joyful. What kept you going through all that?"

She paused—for a long time. At first I thought she might not have understood my question. Then she looked at me and slowly, with great determination, holding my gaze as if she wanted every word to count for the rest of my life, said:

"The... Lord... will... provide!"

This was her final four-word testimony. She did not always have an easy road. She did not always get healed. She did not always get what she wanted. Like everyone else she had to navigate this broken world with its heartaches and disappointments. But she saw the Lord's hand through it all. She became permeated with this perspective, and it sustained her.

That kind of simple trust is the heart of faith. Jerry K. Rose calls this "bedrock faith" because it's very basic, yet set on a deep foundation that is never shaken. We live in such a complicated world. We need to recover simple, bedrock faith: trust in God's unchangeable character.

You may be tempted to place your trust in pastors, pollsters, or professors; scientists or celebrities; teachers or talk show hosts. You may trust your doctor or portfolio or spouse. You may be inclined to trust your own feelings or plans.

I get it. It's gratifying to have a trustworthy physician or a happy marriage or a sense of well-being. But the day may come when even those things falter. So place your ultimate trust exclusively in God.

That's what Hebrews 11:6 is all about. Let's skip there for a second.

> "And without faith it is impossible to please God, because anyone who comes to him must believe that he exists and that he rewards those who earnestly seek him." (Hebrews 11:6)

He exists. He rewards. God is real. God is responsive.

Not too complicated, is it? Yet that is the kind of faith that got my mother through all those intense trials. And not just my Mom. Over several decades as a pastor I have noticed that the people in our church who get through trauma with their hope intact are not always the ones with the deepest Bible knowledge. It's the ones with simple, bedrock faith that God is real and God is good.

So in this book I want to make faith simple without being simplistic.

Part of the challenge is that most languages don't really have a good word to translate the biblical idea of faith, so we either make it too theologically complicated or we reduce it to mere positive thinking.

When someone says "faith" in a religious context, we usually imagine it means:
Doctrine
Traditions
Truths to which I assent.

When someone says "faith" in a cultural context, we usually think of it as:
Optimism
Magical thinking
Seeing the bright side.

But in the context of the Hebrew Bible (the Old Testament), faith in God means: **trusting God enough to take the next step.** In the New Testament, "faith" (*pistis* in the original Greek) means: **a commitment to, a trust in, a reliance upon.**

My wife Laurie likes the word *entrustment*. Faith is not about eliminating every last doubt. It's not about understanding every doctrinal nuance. It's not about feeling constant mystical emotion. It's about *trusting*.

Trusting God enough to take action.
Trusting God enough to go his direction.
Trusting God enough to release my worries.

I like that because my *beliefs* can waver.
I can experience doubt.
I can wonder if I have it all exactly right.

And my *emotions* can waver.
I can feel down.
I can feel tired.

But through all that I can still *trust* God. I can "believe He exists and He rewards those who earnestly seek Him." Faith starts with that choice.

Don't miss this: In context, the author of Hebrews is making the case that, long before Christianity or Judaism, *this is all people knew*. They didn't have the revelation that we enjoy in Scripture. But they trusted this. God is real. God is good. So they moved forward in obedience.

When faith is defined merely as rules and doctrine, it produces:
I should.

When faith is defined merely as optimism, it produces:
I could.

But when faith is defined biblically, it produces:
I will.

Because
He is.

That is living faith forward.

5
the rewards
of faith
part 1

...and he rewards those who earnestly seek him.

(Hebrews 11:6)

Faith is always rewarded by God.

God is a personal, loving, gracious God eager to reward those who seek Him. *Anyone* who seeks Him. Always.

This is an ironclad promise throughout the Bible:

> "The LORD searches every heart and understands every desire and every thought. If you seek him, he will be found by you." (1 Chronicles 28:9)

> "Those who seek me find me." (Proverbs 8:17b)

> "You will seek me and find me when you seek me with all your heart." (Jeremiah 29:13)

> "… the one who seeks finds." (Luke 11:10)

> "…whoever believes in him shall not perish but have eternal life." (John 3:16b)

And here in Hebrews 11:

> "He rewards those who diligently seek him."
> (Hebrews 11:6b)

I used to think it was more biblical to follow God without any desire for reward. But Hebrews 11:6 says it's not just *okay* to believe God will reward you. It's part of the kind of faith God is *looking* for.

Jesus directly complimented people for their faith just eight times. What do you see in their stories that can give you a clue about the kind of faith Jesus loves?

• Two blind men follow Jesus all the way into a private home and request healing. Jesus says, "According to your faith it will be done to you" and instantly their sight is restored. (Matthew 9:27-31)

• A Canaanite woman persists in asking Jesus to heal her daughter, even over the objections of Jesus' disciples. He exclaims, "Woman, you have great faith! Your request is granted!" (Matthew 15:21-28)

• Four men can't get their paralyzed friend past the crowds to see Jesus, so they lower him through a hole they bash in the roof. When Jesus "saw their faith," he forgives the man's sins and heals him. (Mark 2:1-12)

• A woman with hemophilia thinks, "If I can just touch Jesus' robe, I'll be healed." She pushes through a thick crowd and brushes her fingers against his cloak. "Daughter, your faith has healed you" Jesus tells her. (Mark 5:25-34)

• A blind beggar loudly asks Jesus to heal him, even though people tell him to shut up. Jesus says, "Your faith has healed you." (Mark 10:46-52)

• A Roman centurion humbly asks for long-distance healing for his servant. Jesus says, "I tell you the truth, I have not found such great faith even in Israel!" (Luke 7:2-10)

• A woman "who had lived a sinful life" rushes into a fancy dinner party to see Jesus, and as the elite guests look on in disapproval, she weeps in gratitude at his feet. Jesus responds, "Your faith has saved you. God in peace." (Luke 7:36-50)

• Jesus heals ten lepers; just one (the only Samaritan) returns and thanks him. Jesus is astonished and says, "Your faith has made you well." (Luke 17:11-19)

These eight instances are the *only* times Jesus compliments someone's faith. What do they all have in common?

As Blaine Smith points out, these people only had an elementary grasp of who Jesus was, so he wasn't impressed with their developed theology (although of course theology is important). But they all had "an uncanny optimism about the possibility of receiving help from Him".

They had two crucial attitudes:

I believe I will benefit by seeking help from Jesus.

I am determined to do whatever is necessary to draw closer to him.

In most cases these people had to overcome significant obstacles to even reach Christ. But they took initiative and were persistent.

So as we begin this journey, two questions.

Do you believe there are substantial benefits to seeking Jesus?

Are you willing to take initiative to spend time with Jesus, as were all these people?

That is the kind of faith God is looking for. Not complicated, is it? Yet it is extremely powerful.

I loved the way Liz Bishop, who worked in our church office for many years, once brilliantly summarized how faith thinks. She hung a homemade sign above the interior door of our church office, so our staff would see it any time we left to face the world outside. It read:

"Eager expectation."

That's it. Faith has eager expectation that God will work.

As Paul David Tripp puts it, "Faith does not just mean you *believe* in God's existence. It means you *live as though you believe* in God's existence; as though you believe, as the writer puts it, 'God rewards those who seek him.'"

So I challenge you. Seek God during this study. *Eagerly* expect that he will reward you.

That is living faith forward.

6
the rewards
of faith
part 2

...he rewards those who earnestly seek him.

(Hebrews 11:6)

**Faith is a necessity.
Woe to him who believes in nothing.
– Victor Hugo**

Ok, so the Bible says faith has its rewards. What does science say? You might be surprised to know that around 400 papers are published each year on this topic.

It's hard to measure "faith," so researchers have to look at quantifiable activities that tend to correlate with faith, like church attendance.

• According to the L.A. Times, an analysis of 42 studies published in the journal *Health Psychology* found that people with religious involvement live longer.

• A study at the University of Pittsburgh Medical Center showed that improvements in life expectancy of those who attend weekly religious services are comparable with those who exercise regularly! (Now imagine if you both exercised *and* went to church!)

• An MIT study found regular church attenders have lower rates of divorce and welfare dependency.

• Another study showed strong correlation between church attendance and better sleep. (I know! I see you out there every time I preach!)

• Regular church attenders tend to experience less depression. Researchers believe this may be attributed to the social support offered by churches.

• Another study concluded the most sexually satisfied couples are those who worship together on a weekly basis.

Longer life. Less depression. Better health. Better sleep. Better sex. Those are good rewards!

Even atheists are noticing the correlation.

In a fascinating column about the effect of Christianity in Africa, well-known atheist Matthew Parris wrote,

> "It confounds my ideological beliefs, stubbornly refuses to fit my world view, and has embarrassed my belief that there is no God. Now a confirmed atheist, I've become convinced… Christianity changes people's hearts. It brings a spiritual transformation. The rebirth is real. The change is good. Far from having cowed or confined its converts, their faith appears to have liberated and relaxed them. Christianity, with its teaching of a direct, personal, two-way link between the individual and God, unsubordinate to any other human being... liberates."

Put it all together and a pattern seems to emerge: We simply run better on faith.

So let's start putting some more of that fuel in your tank.

7
faith fueled
by awe

By faith we understand that the universe was formed at God's command...

(Hebrews 11:3a)

Belief is a wise wager. – Blaise Pascal

Famous scientist Stephen Hawking wrote "The Grand Design" to defend his atheism. Ironically, the book had the exact opposite effect on me.

In his first chapter Hawking writes, "The discovery recently of the extreme fine-tuning of so many laws of nature could lead some to the idea that this grand design is the work of some grand Designer…" In fact, he says, if you try to explain how this all happened by accident, you run into literally impossible odds. There is simply not a chance that this happened by chance! Hawking goes on to handle the problem of God this way: why not postulate an infinite number of *multiverses*?

Another famous scientist, Paul Davies, wrote his response to this idea in the New York Times: "The multiverse theory is increasingly popular, but it doesn't so much explain as dodge the whole issue. Where do *they* come from?"

What I get out of this debate is simple. The odds against *anything* being alive *anywhere* in this universe are so great that the mere fact that you and I are reading these words, thinking about this together, is less likely than you winning every lottery in history.

The Bible's explanation: God is the creative powerhouse behind everything, the artist-engineer-poet-scientist who wove it all together.

> "By faith we understand that the universe was formed at God's command…" (Hebrews 11:3)

Freeman Dyson was a Princeton professor famed for his work in quantum mechanics and astrophysics. He observed,

> "The more I examine the universe and the details of its architecture, the more evidence I find that the universe in some sense must have known we were coming…"

John Polkinghorne was professor of mathematical physics at Cambridge and an expert in quantum physics. He concluded,

> "The universe is the expression of the purposive design of a Creator, who has endowed it with the finely tuned potentiality for life."

Mathematical genius Blaise Pascal argued that faith was a worthy gamble:

> "Belief is a wise wager. Granted that faith cannot be proved, what harm will come to you if you gamble on its truth and it proves false? If you gain, you gain all; if you lose, you lose nothing. Wager, then, without hesitation, that He exists."

Plus, we run better on belief. Researchers are learning our brains work better when we have moments of awe each day. Even 20 minutes of focus on something beautiful produces measurable improvement in emotional health and cognitive ability. I can't think of a better source of awe than worship of God.

So put aside some moments today to consider the sheer greatness of God's creative power.

Take in the trees and the sun and the clouds and the water.

Think of the unimaginably small odds of your own existence. Breathe. Say, "Thank you."

That's step one to living faith forward.

8
faith is seeing the yet unseen

...what is seen was not made out of what was visible.

(Hebrews 11:3b)

**Faith is to believe what you do not see;
the reward is to see what you believe. – Augustine**

When my grandfather Gustav was born in 1896, so much that
we see every day was still unseen by anyone. I looked it up.
When he was a baby, there were:

• No airplanes
• No plastic
• No escalators
• No safety razors
• No radios
• No air conditioners
• No teddy bears
• No crayons
• No teabags
• No cornflakes
• No mass-market automobiles
• No movies
• No toasters
• No Band-Aids
• No frozen meals
• No spiral-bound notebooks
• No TV

And of course no computers, WiFi, cable, or internet.
No Pixar, no Disney, no Marvel, no iPhones.

All these things we see now, and take for granted,were
unseen. Unknown. Unimagined.

That's one of the points the author to the Hebrews is making.
What is now *seen* was once *unseen*. Every single thing.

So when the readers of Hebrews are struggling to continue in their faith because they see little instant payoff, no visible signs of progress, no social acceptance, well, that's how everything great started. That's how the Jewish faith started. That's how the universe started. That's how *everything* *ever* started. To these struggling young Christians whose imagination is faltering and whose confidence is fading, the author is saying, our little movement is the start of something great!

Many Christians feel they are faltering today too.
Covid is cutting into church attendance.
Culture is cutting into church acceptance.
Crises are devastating people's mental health.
Sometimes it seems there's not much positive to see.

That means this is a perfect time for us to practice what we believe. Now is not the time to disband or disengage. Now is the time to stick together and endure. It's easy to live out your faith when you can see what's next, you can pay your bills, you have good health, society shares your values. But do you believe because you can see all these blessings or do you believe in what you cannot now see?

On the days you look at yourself, your children, your church, your ministry, your community, and feel discouraged by what is *visible*-- the lack of growth, the immaturity, the problems, remember this: Jesus said even the kingdom of God starts like a tiny seed. You can barely see it now. But it will grow.

Farmers keep farming though the seeds haven't sprouted.
Artists keep dreaming though the picture isn't painted.

Authors keep plotting though the book isn't written. Believers keep believing though the kingdom isn't fully manifested.

Because God is an expert at starting stuff out of... *nothing*.

9
ex nihilo

...so that what is seen was not made out of what was visible.

(Hebrews 11:3b)

Faith understands everything began from nothing.

Let's think about this again: God created everything that ever existed out of *absolutely nothing*.

He didn't start with a blank canvas, or lump of clay, or a sheet of paper.

There was *zero*.

Theologians have a Latin name for this: *ex nihilo*, which literally means "out of nothing".

This is a kind of creative power I have a hard time fathoming, because there isn't anything we humans make on our planet like that. You and I always start with previously existing materials in order to make something else. Like Carl Sagan said, "If you wish to truly make an apple pie from scratch, you must first create the universe."

Only God creates from scratch.

When the Bible says, "In the beginning God created the heavens and the earth," (Genesis 1:1) the Hebrew word used there for *created* is *bara*. It's only used in the Old Testament when *God* creates.

When *humans* create, there's another, lesser Hebrew word used. It's intended to express that, while our creativity reflects our creative God, we can't really produce *something out of nothing* the way God can.

This is not just limited to the way God makes stars and

planets. This is also how God changes *you*.

God is not held back by pre-existing conditions. He can do anything from scratch, when there are no resources, no hope, nothing.

Nihilo.

I think of the stories of some friends of mine.

Kurtis was smoking pot for breakfast, lunch, and dinner. He didn't want to feel any pain; he didn't want to feel anything at all. His once well-muscled construction workers' body had been laid waste by Multiple Sclerosis. His marriage? Over. His career skills? Useless. He was being warehoused in a nursing home for low-income patients, feeling no good to anyone. Like a big zero.

Nihilo.

One day Kurtis slipped out of the facility, steered his motorized wheelchair to the edge of a busy street, and tried to pick out a big car so he could roll into its path and end his suffering. But his nerve failed him and he rolled back to his room.

Then a friend invited him to church. And from the first day Kurtis felt something stirring— something alive, happy, playful, all around him. He told me he believed it was the Holy Spirit breathing new life into his dead soul.

The way I knew Kurtis, worshipping at church with tears flowing, leading the residents' advocacy group at the nursing center, greeting people at church with the biggest grin in the building, was nothing like the ruined man he says he once was.

Then there's Robert. He went into the family business several years ago: Importing and exporting… drugs. With no trace of conscience, he happily funneled millions of dollars of drugs, mostly cocaine, into the U.S. It was a booming market. Until he got busted and sent to prison. And his marriage crumbled. And his daughter was murdered. And he lost everything. He was left with *nothing*.

Nihilo.

But tiny seeds planted in Robert as a child began to finally take root as he attended prison Bible studies. The man I know smiles more than almost anyone else at church. His occupation? He's a counselor. His specialty? Addictions. Helping others get off the path he once walked. God looked at his total darkness and said, "Let there be light." And Robert *shines*.

Next time you see someone and think, "There is no hope there—nothing", remember how God likes to work.

Ex nihilo.

Seeing that is part of living faith forward.

10
it's always been faith

By faith Abel brought God a better offering than Cain did. By faith he was commended as righteous, when God spoke well of his offerings. And by faith Abel still speaks, even though he is dead.

(Hebrews 11:4)

Faith knows: It's not about me.

Now the plot explodes.
The rest of Hebrews 11 is one great story after another.

And we start with a verse that ruined my life. No kidding. It haunted every religious step I took, for many years.

The story happens very early in the book of Genesis. Abel is a shepherd. His brother Cain is a farmer.

> "When it was time for the harvest, Cain presented some of his crops as a gift to the LORD. Abel also brought a gift—the best portions of the firstborn lambs from his flock. The LORD accepted Abel and his gift, but he did not accept Cain and his gift." (Genesis 4:3-5a)

What's all that about?
Does God reject vegetarians?
Loves BBQ, hates soy?
Moral of the story, "blood offering good; plant offering bad"?

As a teen I heard exactly that. Abel somehow cracked the mystery of what God wanted. A blood sacrifice. Cain got it wrong. God rejected him.

So God, to me, became the unpredictably prickly deity who never revealed His will but expected you to follow it anyway. I became worried that if somehow, even by mistake, I prayed wrong or believed wrong or acted wrong, I would be driven out like Cain.

When my life seemed to go badly, or I couldn't feel a sense of God's blessing, I always concluded I must be doing something that annoyed the Lord. So I tried a "better sacrifice": kneeling while praying, reading the Bible in a harder translation, going on a more intense mission trip. Maybe that would finally be the offering God would "speak well of." But who knew? I longed to be Abel but was terrified I was Cain.

I see now this is exactly the opposite of the point.

It's a mistake to read into the Genesis account any hidden reasons for God's acceptance of Abel's offering and rejection of Cain's. The writer of Genesis is silent about the reason. One thing we can say for sure: It is not about meat or veggies.

Because all through the Bible we see offerings exactly like Cain's accepted—and even commanded:

> "As you harvest your crops, bring the very best of the first harvest to the house of the LORD your God." (Exodus 23:19 NLT)

And we see animal offerings like Abel's rejected:

> "What makes you think I want all your sacrifices?" says the LORD. "I am sick of your burnt offerings of rams and the fat of fattened cattle." (Isaiah 1:11 NLT)

So what was it about Abel's offering? In Hebrews we get the answer. Did you catch it? It's repeated three times:

> "By *faith* Abel brought God a better offering...by *faith* he was commended as righteous...by *faith* Abel still speaks..."

Abel came to God in *faith*.

As Bible scholar F.F. Bruce put it, "Sacrifice is acceptable to God not because of its material content, but insofar as it is the outward expression of a devoted heart." Abel was focused on God. Cain was focused on his works. The giveaway is Cain's response. He is not happy for Abel. He is furious.

> "This made Cain very angry, and he looked dejected… And while they were in the field, Cain attacked his brother, Abel, and killed him." (Genesis 4:5b,8)

Cain was poisoned by his injured pride.

Want to be Abel and not Cain? The writer to the Hebrews is reminding these early Christians, who seem to long for the spectacle of a temple with its dramatic sacrifices and beautiful ritual, it's not really about that. It's never been about that. Long before Judaism, long before Christianity, people were saved the same exact way they are saved now. Not by the ritual. By faith.

> "For it is by grace you have been saved, through faith— and this is not from yourselves, it is the gift of God— not by works, so that no one can boast." (Ephesians 2:8,9)

Cain wanted to boast. Abel just wanted to worship.

Which one are you?

11
faith is a
daily walk

By faith Enoch was taken from this life, so that he did not experience death: 'He could not be found, because God had taken him away.' For before he was taken, he was commended as one who pleased God.

(Hebrews 11:5)

Faith means walking the walk, one step at a time.

It was an unexpected challenge picking up my friend Bill Butterworth at the airport today for the first time since the Covid crisis. Because I did not recognize him. I knew he was at baggage claim but for the life of me I could not see him. He has lost so much weight, and put on so much muscle, he looks like a new man.

I was astonished. How did he do it? He told me he got a new, very enthusiastic, very direct doctor who asked him about his exercise routine.

Bill replied, "Well, I try to walk 45 minutes a couple times a week."

His doctor poked him in the chest with each of his words. "You only need EIGHT minutes of walking a DAY! But do it. Every. Single. Day!"

So that's what Bill did. Every day. Eight minutes. Of course most days those eight minutes turned into 30 or more. A year and a half year later, he's got a different body.

That's the power of a daily walk. Starts small. But it can get you someplace. Even if you start later in life. Like Bill. And Enoch.

The Genesis account implies that for the first 65 years of his life, Enoch did *not* walk with God.

> "When Enoch had lived 65 years, he became the father of Methuselah. And after he became the father

of Methuselah, Enoch walked faithfully with God…"
(Genesis 5:21,22)

A baby cried. And a dad's life took a U-turn.

He *walked* with God.

Now this is huge. You may think you've heard that metaphor before but pour yourself another cup of coffee and just think it over a minute.

What's a "walk"? Picture it.

Got it? What do you see? Whether you imagine a bounce or a shuffle or a glide, all walks have this in common: Slow and steady progress in a certain direction, one step at a time. A walk gets somewhere. But very incrementally.

Enoch is an example of what the writer of Hebrews longs to see happen to his readers: Steady, slow, incremental growth in faith. One day at a time. Every. Single. Day. That gets you somewhere.

In fact the Genesis account suggests Enoch's walk with God grew so intimate, so personal, so deep, that one day he just sort of faded from this world to the next.

> "Enoch walked faithfully with God; then he was no more, because God took him away." (Genesis 5:24)

I haven't seen it happen quite this miraculously, but I have seen people so close to God in their daily walk that death is just a transition into the presence of the One who is their daily companion. My own father's final words as he lay dying of cancer were, "It's like a dream…God is all around me." Then he died. I think he saw the hospital room, closed his eyes, and when he opened them again he saw Jesus.

Enoch reminds you and me: We're all walking somewhere. Each choice I make, each thought I entertain, each voice I listen to, is a step. Where are your steps taking you?

It's not too late to change direction. Like Enoch, the catalyst may be the birth of a child. Or a move to a new city, or a cancer diagnosis, or marriage trouble. All these life events can be an opportunity to look up and see where you're headed. Don't like it? Make a U-turn. Seem like an impossible change? Just take that first step.

Maybe that means seeing a marriage counselor.
Starting a daily habit of prayer and meditation.
Starting to attend church again.
Going to that first meeting.
Joining a small group.
Volunteering.

Or taking the very first step of faith into a new life by trusting Jesus Christ as your Lord and Savior.
One thing's for sure. You can't reach your destination all at once. Faith is a walk. It starts with one step in the right direction.

And one day at a time, one moment at a time, amazing things can happen. As our next hero discovered.

12
faith that
keeps going

By faith Noah, when warned about things not yet seen, in holy fear built an ark to save his family. By his faith he condemned the world and became heir of the righteousness that is in keeping with faith.

(Hebrews 11:7)

**Faith does not make things easy.
It makes them possible.**

Dashrath Manjhi was born into a family at the lowest level of India's caste system. In 1959 his wife Falguni Devi was injured in a fall and died on the way to the hospital because the narrow trail from their remote mountain village snaked 34 miles to the closest hospital. They could not get to a doctor quickly enough.

Manjhi resolved to honor his wife by cutting a roadway through the ridge to make his village more accessible. He had no funds. No tools except a chisel. But he set to work.

In 1982, the roadway he built with his own hands was finally completed. It took him almost 23 years, but he single-handedly reduced the distance between his village and the hospital from 34 miles to ten. And it's not just some footpath. It's a modern concrete roadway.

How did he persevere? He said, "When I started hammering the hill, people called me a lunatic—but that just steeled my resolve."

Manjhi's story reminds me of someone else who started a long, strange construction project single-handedly. He's next in the Hebrews Hall of Fame of Faith. Noah.

Typically when I teach on Noah, I'm instantly derailed by questions. "Wait, an ark? Are you serious? How big was it? Was this really a world-wide flood?" And any actual life lessons that could be learned from Noah's story are lost in computations about the size of his boat.

So I want to ask a different question: What is the point of this story?

It starts in Genesis 6. The wickedness of humans is so great that God decides to judge the world.

> "But Noah found grace in the eyes of the Lord."
> (Genesis 6:8)

This is the first place grace is mentioned in the Bible. Noah was not perfect, or he would not have needed grace. Later, Noah gets so drunk on wine from his own vineyard that he collapses naked in public and two of his sons have to cover him up and take him inside. So, perfect? No. But he found God's grace.

And in response to God's favor, Noah shows three qualities of faith:

• **Noah was different.**

Faith swims upstream. Noah was not perfect but he was not afraid to speak up or stand out.

> "Noah was a righteous man, blameless among the people of his time, and he walked faithfully with God."
> (Genesis 6:9)

• **Noah was obedient.**

Noah followed God's instructions. Even when they seemed super weird.

> "Noah did everything just as God commanded him."
> (Genesis 6:22)

· Noah was persistent.

The Bible says it took Noah 120 years to build the ark. Question: Even if you really wanted to be used by God, could you maintain enthusiasm for a project that was going to take your entire life? Rick Warren points out three things that will tempt you to give up.

Problems: Every good idea has something wrong with it.

Pressures: Noah must have thought, "All of the weight of the world on one man? It's too much to handle!"

People: People will disappoint you. People will misunderstand you. People will criticize you.

I've been tempted to quit my own ministry at times for precisely these three reasons. But I don't want to let my decisions be dictated by problems, pressures, or people. I only want to be dictated to by God.

After his death, Dashrath Manjhi became an Indian hero; a postage stamp honoring him was released by the government of India in December 2016. Noah is a hero now too. But it took years of perseverance.

This is exactly the point of his story in Hebrews 11. Keep going, the author is saying. It may feel to you like the whole idea of building a new community in Christ, the whole idea of church, is a giant failed project. Maybe like the first readers of Hebrews, you're tired of trying the Christian thing. You've seen Christians fail. You've felt the abuse. You just want to quit. What's the use?

Keep building that road. Keep building that ark. Keep building that church.

The church you're part of can be an ark of safety for people who would otherwise drown. There will come a time when what you are building now, one plank at a time, is needed.

Faith does not make the task easy. Faith makes it possible. So stay on task. Don't give up.

That is living faith forward.

13
the link between faith and risk

By faith Abraham, when called to go to
a place he would later receive as his
inheritance, obeyed and went, even though
he did not know where he
was going.

(Hebrews 11:8)

**Failure is not the greatest risk.
The greatest risk is never trying.**

The story of Abraham is set more than 2,000 years before
Jesus was born, roughly 4,000 years ago. Humans were just
developing the very first civilizations in the very first cities.
Abraham is from one of those places, the city of Ur in Sumer.

Pretty cool place. Around his time the Sumerians rapidly
invented:

• Writing
• Farming
• Cities
• Bricks
• Metallurgy
• Irrigation
• Chariots
• Mass-produced pottery
• Beer

Sumer had it going on. It was prosperous, protected, perfect.

Then God tells Abraham to leave.

And even though he is not told where to go,
how far to go,
how long it will take,
or how we will know when he gets there,
Abraham risks everything and leaves.
Trades buildings and beer for tents and well water.
The original leap of faith.

"By faith he dwelt in the promised land as a stranger in a foreign country. He lived in tents, as did Isaac and Jacob, who were heirs with him of the same promise. For he was looking forward to the city with foundations, whose architect and builder is God." (Hebrews 11:9,10)

Psychologist Richard Wiseman has done fascinating work on luck. Is it true that some people are just lucky, while others are unlucky? He followed the lives of 400 people for 10 years (he found them after he placed ads in newspapers asking for people who thought of themselves as very lucky or very unlucky).

Those who saw themselves as "lucky" did indeed have more good things happen to them. Why? They risked more. And failed more often. But they shrugged it off and tried something else. Because they tried more stuff, it was more probable good things would happen. People who saw themselves as "unlucky" craved security and were more anxious. So they tried less. As a result, they missed out on many opportunities.

People of faith could learn a lesson from the "lucky." There is a definite link between faith and risk.

Jesus told a parable specifically about this. After two servants take risks with their master's resources and report a profit on their investments,

"...the last servant said, 'Master, I know you have high standards... I was afraid I might disappoint you, so I found a good hiding place and secured your money.

Here it is, safe and sound down to the last cent.' The master was furious. 'That's a terrible way to live! It's criminal to live cautiously like that!'"
(Matthew 25:24-26 The Message)

Jesus is critical of those who never take faith risks. If we're afraid to risk anything, very little good will be accomplished.

True confessions: I am not a natural risk-taker. But I have discovered that adventurous, risk-taking faith—for the kingdom of God—is rewarding! That's something I have *grown into*, not something I was *born with*.

In fact, this kind of faith is a gift from God that he is eager to give you. Will you ask?

Try this prayer: *Lord, help me move out more adventurously in faith as Abraham did. Help me remember failure is not the greatest risk. The greatest risk is never trying.*

Faith moves forward.

14
faith laughs

And by faith even Sarah, who was past childbearing age, was enabled to bear children because she considered him faithful who had made the promise. And so from this one man, and he as good as dead, came descendants as numerous as the stars in the sky and as countless as the sand on the seashore.

(Hebrews 11:11,12)

Faith allows for the possibility of joy.

When we last left Abram and his wife Sarah, God had called
them to leave their comfortable city home in Ur and move
to a new land, sight unseen. God promised they will be the
ancestors of a great nation.

Now it's 24 years later. It's been quite a trip.

When Abram arrives in the land God calls him to settle in
forever, there's a famine, and Abram turns right around and
heads for Egypt. He asks Sarah to lie and say she's his sister,
then raises no objection when Pharoah brings her into his
harem. After Pharoah realizes Sarah's already married he
sends her back. Then Sarah and Abram then both mistreat
their Egyptian slave Hagar horribly when she becomes
pregnant with Abram's child.

Oh, and one more big problem: Abram and Sarah still have
no children together. And are a LOT older. As you read this
story in the Bible, you're meant to be thinking, "Why in the
world did God choose these people? It is not working. They
are inconsistent and incapable."

People who never read the Bible imagine it's full of simplistic
morality tales, all about good guys versus bad guys. But
when you actually dig into it, you realize it's as nuanced as
the most sophisticated modern drama. It's not about churchy
people consistently doing correct things. It's about normal
people consistently blowing it—and God redeeming them.
Over and over.

God's response to Abram's repeated inconsistencies? He reaffirms his promise.

It's enough to make you laugh. Abram and Sarah sure thought so.

When God *again* tells Abram he will be the father of many nations (God even changes his name to "Abraham" which means "father of a multitude") and that Sarah would be the mother, Abraham falls on his face and loses it.

Usually in the Bible when someone falls face down in the dust they're pleading for their life. But here Abraham just laughs. He thinks:

> "Can a child be born to a man who is a hundred years old? Can Sarah give birth at the age of ninety?" (Genesis 17:17)

Later still, the Lord appears to Abraham *again* (we, the readers, are told it is the Lord, but Abraham sees what looks like three men). After he welcomes them to his tent, one of the three speaks. Sarah is listening at the tent door.

> "I will surely return to you about this time next year, and Sarah your wife will have a son." (Genesis 18:10)

And Sarah laughs.

I've always wondered about that laugh. Was it a chortle? Cackle? Howl? Blast? A guffaw, like "You have GOT to be kidding me!?" A crooked smile of polite disbelief, "Me, a mom? Don't think so." A sad chuckle while shaking her head,

"I have heard THIS one before." Maybe a little of everything. So God adds,

> "Why did Sarah laugh? Is anything impossible for the LORD? At the appointed time I will come back to you, and in about a year she will have a son."
> (Genesis 18:14 CSB)

The scene fades with Sarah denying that she laughed, and the Lord saying, "Oh yes you did."

Fade up. Same tent door. One year later.

A baby cries. Sarah has just given birth to a son. She names him Isaac. Which means… "laughter."

I think Sarah had a sense of self-deprecating humor. Her incredulous laughter of disbelief has turned into a satisfied smile of joy at God's wonderful grace.

"Is anything impossible for the LORD?" That's a faith lesson heard again and again throughout the pages of the Bible.

God reassures the Israelites centuries later that they will return to the land, asking,

> "Is anything too hard for me?" (Jeremiah 32:27b)

A young virgin named Mary is told she will bear a son,

> "For nothing will be impossible with God."
> (Luke 1:37 ESV)

Her son grows up and says:

> "Humanly speaking, it is impossible. But not with God. Everything is possible with God." (Mark 10:27 NLT)

Maybe laughter feels like it's a long way off for you. Jesus has a pleasant promise:

> "Blessed are you who weep now, for you will laugh." (Luke 6:21)

Ever feel you're too bad for God to bless? Too lost for God to love? Too old or tired or weak for God to use? Like the whole idea of a God who might choose and cherish someone like you is, well, a joke? Abraham and Sarah would say, "Tell me about it! But just wait. Nothing is impossible for God."

Are you open to that? Dare to let faith work on your crooked smirk of disbelief and slowly turn it into a wide smile of delight. Believe there's laughter ahead.

That's living faith forward.

15
faith sees the far country

All these people were still living by faith when they died. They did not receive the things promised; they only saw them and welcomed them from a distance, admitting that they were foreigners and strangers on earth. People who say such things show that they are looking for a country of their own. If they had been thinking of the country they had left, they would have had opportunity to return. Instead, they were longing for a better country—a heavenly one.

(Hebrews 11:13-16a)

Faith in heaven feeds hope on earth.

In *The Lord of the Rings*, the hobbit Sam makes a speech to his tired friend Frodo that sounds like a summary of these Hebrews 11 heroes (this is the movie version of the speech):

> "It's like in the great stories, Mr. Frodo. The ones that really mattered. Full of darkness and danger they were. And sometimes you didn't want to know the end… because how could the end be happy? How could the world go back to the way it was when so much bad had happened? But in the end, it's only a passing thing… this shadow. Even darkness must pass. A new day will come. And when the sun shines it will shine out the clearer…"

Maybe you feel you're in the middle of such a story right now.
You are facing discouragement.
You are fighting hopelessness.
You feel like giving up.

As Sam goes on to say:

> "Folk in those stories had lots of chances of turning back, only they didn't. Because they were holding on to something."

We know the folk in all these great Hebrews 11 stories felt like turning back, because the Bible records their hesitations. So why didn't they? Hebrews 11 tells us:

> "They were longing for a better country—a heavenly one." (Hebrews 11:16a)

They believed they were getting somewhere.

In one of the earliest scenes in The Lord of the Rings novels, Frodo has a dream, a powerful vision of a paradise, a "far green country" beyond this world of darkness. Then a thousand pages later, in one of the final chapters, he gets a glimpse again:

> "(Frodo) smelled a sweet fragrance on the air and heard the sound of singing that came over the water. And then it seemed to him that as in his dream...the grey rain-curtain turned all to silver glass and was rolled back, and he beheld white shores and beyond them a far green country under a swift sunrise."

That vision of a better land, even if glimpsed only briefly in an elusive dream, is part of what keeps him going. When you get a vision of the future God has planned, it can inspire you to endure too.

It's not comfortable to feel like "foreigners and strangers on earth." We want to find a "country of our own" here and now, a place where everyone likes us and is like us. Sociologists say people in the US right now are sorting themselves in a way they never have before, moving to places they feel comfortably similar to their neighbors. I'm not here to tell you where to live, but we all need to be careful not to seek on earth what we will only get in glory. It takes faith to embrace that displaced "foreigners and strangers" feeling. It helps to imagine the far green country.

Part of the problem: Many Christians have only a vague understanding of the Bible's teaching about heaven. So let's roll back the grey curtain for a glimpse:

> "Then I saw a new heaven and a new earth... He will

wipe every tear from their eyes. There will be no more death or mourning or crying or pain, for the old order of things has passed away." He who was seated on the throne said, 'I am making everything new!'"
(Revelation 21:1,4-5a)

Think of the things you love here. They're there. Rivers. Trees. Rainbows. Animals. Loved ones. Delicious food. Music.
Made new.

Think of the things you hate here. They're gone. No more loneliness. No more pandemics. No more disasters.
No more injustice.

In Hebrews 11, the fact that these people all longed for someplace better is taken as strong evidence that there must be such a place. C.S. Lewis made this argument too. He pointed out that we hunger for food, because food exists. We thirst for water, because water exists. Why would we long for heaven, for paradise, for a better place, if it was not real — somewhere?

> "If we find ourselves with a desire that nothing in this world can satisfy, the most probable explanation is that we were made for another world." - C.S. Lewis

So don't give up. There is a "far green country."
Like The Apostle Paul says:

> "I consider that our present sufferings are not worth comparing with the glory that will be revealed in us."
> (Romans 8:18)

Trusting *that* is living faith forward.

16
faith when all seems dark

By faith Abraham, when God tested him, offered Isaac as a sacrifice. He who had embraced the promises was about to sacrifice his one and only son, even though God had said to him, "It is through Isaac that your offspring will be reckoned." Abraham reasoned that God could even raise the dead, and so in a manner of speaking he did receive Isaac back from death.

(Hebrews 11:17-19)

Faith believes God will come through.

As my friend David Tieche says in his book on Abraham,

> "More than any other moment or chapter in his life, this story is the one that artists and poets will focus on most often throughout history. This is, for better or worse, the story that will define Abraham's life. Scholars, rabbis, artists, teachers, poets, and readers have tried to make sense of this story for millennia."

It is a tale well told. Almost impossible to stop once you start it. God appears to Abraham for the final time in his life.

> "Take your son, your only son Isaac, whom you love, and go to a mountain I will show you." (Genesis 22:2a)

Then he commands the unimaginable.

> "Sacrifice him there as a burnt offering on a mountain I will show you." (Genesis 22:2b)

Abraham asks Isaac to accompany him to the mountain. "But where is the sacrificial animal?" Isaac asks.

> "Abraham answered, 'God himself will provide the lamb for the burnt offering, my son.' And the two of them went on together." (Genesis 22:8)

The tension builds. We can hardly believe what is happening as we read it. Is God really going to allow Abraham to kill the promised child?

Isaac is bound. The knife is raised. And just as Abraham is

about to sacrifice his only son, an angel stops him. "Do not lay a hand on the boy," he says. "Do not do anything to him."

> "Abraham looked up and there in a thicket he saw a ram caught by its horns. He went over and took the ram and sacrificed it as a burnt offering instead of his son." (Genesis 22:13)

Abraham was right. God himself provided the sacrifice.

But why is this story in the Bible? What is it supposed to teach us?

For one thing, this has served for centuries as the go-to passage for missionaries in cultures where human sacrifice was practiced. And that includes most ancient cultures. The Abraham and Isaac story was God yelling to all our human ancestors, "Stop." Stop forever. From now on, God will provide the sacrifice. I think God made sure it was riveting because he wanted to capture their imaginations. You don't change culture with a boring story.

God himself provided the sacrifice.

The Abraham-and-Isaac story led to the development of the sacrificial system of the Jerusalem temple. Animals were brought there to be laid on the altar in what was almost a reenactment of this story.

Until God himself provided the sacrifice.

Earlier in Hebrews, the author explains.

"It is impossible for the blood of bulls and goats to take away sins… we have been made holy through the sacrifice of the body of Jesus Christ once for all." (Hebrews 10:4,10)

No more ritual sacrifice of *anything* is needed. God is saying, "Stop." Stop forever. The writer of Hebrews is arguing that his readers no longer need the temples and altars of their established religions. They are saved by faith, and this is not new. This is what started it all—faith in God's provision to provide the sacrifice himself. So when they have faith in Jesus as God's provision for them, they are tying into a very ancient idea, an idea that goes all the way back to Abraham.

But as David Tieche points out, modern readers also have another question: How did Abraham survive this ordeal *emotionally*? The text gives us some hints.

First, he tells his servants, "*We* will worship and then we will come back to you." We. Both of us. Abraham believes that somehow God will not violate His previous promise. Isaac is coming back alive.

Second, the author of Hebrews suggests Abraham believed there might even be a *resurrection*. God brought Isaac into the world miraculously. So he figured God could even raise him miraculously.

Simply put: Abraham believed God would come through. He did.

That is living faith forward.

17
faith when i am weak

By faith Isaac blessed Jacob and Esau in regard to their future. By faith Jacob, when he was dying, blessed each of Joseph's sons, and worshiped as he leaned on the top of his staff.

(Hebrews 11:20-21)

Faith believes God is at work even in my weakness.

Looking at the Hebrews 11 list of faith heroes can have an unintended consequence if you're unfamiliar with their backstories. You can take a cursory glance at these names and think, "Obviously I do not compare. I'm no hero. I messed up. I missed my chance. I am living some sad B-movie version of the life God wanted for me."

So you need to know: this list is full of cowards and criminals, scoundrels and scammers, victims and victimizers, people who second-guessed God yet got second chances. You're about to meet some of the most colorful.

Next three portraits in the Hall of Fame of Faith: Isaac, Jacob, and Joseph. But these are not pictures of three men in their prime. The writer of Hebrews chooses to describe them all *as they are dying*.

Why?

I think it's because the earlier years of all three had lots of detours, doubts, and distractions.

Take Isaac. He lived longer than any of the other patriarchs of the nation of Israel, but gets way less space in the pages of the Bible. Abraham, Jacob, and Joseph get 12 chapters each. Isaac? Two. For a child whose birth was foretold by God, he's kind of underwhelming.

God speaks to him in a super-encouraging vision, yet at the earliest sign of possible danger, Isaac runs scared. Some men observe how beautiful his wife is, so like his father before him, he says she is his sister. He figures, if they know he's her husband, they might kill him to get her. Now, there is no indication from these guys that they would ever actually do this. It's all in his mind.

Which brings up a point about faith.

Worry and faith have something in common: They both imagine outcomes that haven't happened yet. Fear pictures a negative future. Faith believes in a positive future. Both make assumptions about things they cannot yet see. So why not choose faith over fear? What do you have to lose but the anxiety that is sabotaging your joy?

Isaac sees scary stuff instead of blessings. But God keeps blessing him anyway. Still he does not go on the journey God assigned him until the Philistines keep filling up his wells with dirt and he is forced to move to find water. Not exactly living faith forward.

In fact Isaac seems almost entirely focused on pleasure and self-preservation. Even when he's about to die, facing eternity, you're reading his story and you're hoping he's going to have a "come to Yahweh" moment, and he's dreaming of DoorDash. He orders his son Esau to "go kill some game and prepare a savory dish for me."

Dad, you're dying, any last words of wisdom?
"Mmmmm. Savory venison."

Not until almost the literal last moment of his life does he finally do what God had asked and blesses the son God had chosen, Jacob. That is the one moment of faith mentioned in Hebrews 12. Reluctant, late, weak faith. And he makes the list.

His son Jacob is a con artist who tries to trick dad out of his brother's inheritance. Later, an angel (or perhaps God himself) shows up in the form of a man to bless him. Instead of receiving the blessing by grace through faith, Jacob instantly concludes he must wrestle the blessing from the angel—and attacks him. Classic.

Like his father, his faith is up and down. Sometimes he gets it and sometimes he forgets it. Sometimes he's faithful and sometimes he's fearful.

But finally, as he is dying, Jacob blesses his sons and two grandsons and says to Joseph, "God will be with you."

These "heroes of the faith" *barely* had faith. Barely obeyed. But they had that tiny mustard seed Jesus talked about later. And God grew it.

I think the writer of Hebrews includes these stories because these guys came back around. Remember, the original readers of Hebrews were people whose confidence is so low some of them are bailing on their faith, drifting away.

So did even these patriarchs. For a while. But in the end they returned.

And that means you can too.

You are still alive. Still breathing. That means you can turn around. You can trust instead of worry, bless instead of scheme, rest instead of wrestle.

To summarize these stories:
Early wanderers. Late bloomers.
Weak saints. Powerful Savior.
Small faith. Big God.

But what about when you are faithful—and everything still falls apart?

18
faith sees obstacles as opportunites

By faith Joseph, when his end was near, spoke about the exodus of the Israelites from Egypt and gave instructions concerning the burial of his bones.

(Hebrews 11:22)

Faith knows God is always at work.

As I write, the San Francisco Giants are having a surprisingly good season. They keep coming back from one setback after another to find ways to win. And that has me thinking of Dave Dravecky.

Beloved by Giants fans, Dave was a popular pitcher until a tumor invaded his throwing arm. After surgery he forged a surprising comeback—then the cancer returned. Dave's career crashed the very day the Giants clinched the pennant on their way to the World Series.

His arm was amputated. Then his influence took off.

Dave and his wife Jan became speakers and authors who have inspired millions, including our congregation, about enduring tough times with faith. One of Dave's favorite Bible verses is Genesis 50:20, "You meant it for evil, but God meant it for good." That verse comes at the very end of the long, strange story of Joseph in the Book of Genesis.

Joseph starts as sort of the classic genius kid with tons of potential but zero social skills. He keeps telling his older brothers how they will bow to him one day, until finally they decide to just get rid of him. They actually sell their own brother into slavery and tell their father he is dead.

One thing after another goes wrong for Joseph: he becomes a slave to an Egyptian, he is falsely accused of a crime, he is thrown into prison, he waits years for exoneration in vain— he gets his hopes up and they are dashed repeatedly—but by God's grace each obstacle turns into an opportunity. In prison, while waiting, and waiting, and waiting, he serves those in need. His talent is spotted and he eventually rises through the ranks until he is advisor to Pharoah.

Then during a famine his brothers come begging for help. They do not recognize him. He looks and sounds Egyptian. At first he toys with them, threatening them. Finally he reveals his identity and agrees to assist.

That's when Joseph says it.

"You meant it for evil, but God meant it for good."

Because of their brutal betrayal, he ended up in a place of power. Now he can save their lives.

Joseph discovered a key to serenity: God takes even misbehavior and misunderstandings and rewrites them into a great story.

I don't love the saying, "Everything happens for a reason." That makes it sound like God purposely plans evil in order to turn it into good. The Bible teaches God is not the author of evil. Maybe a better way to say it is, "God uses everything for his purposes." Or, "God turns obstacles into opportunities." Or, "God never wastes a hurt."

That is definitely true.

As he is dying, Joseph reminds his brothers, "I am about to die, but God will surely take care of you, and bring you back from this land to the land he promised..." (Genesis 50:24)

The brothers are now afraid of losing him, their protector. And indeed, a Pharoah arises who "knew not Joseph" and their descendants are enslaved. Tough times are ahead. But Joseph has seen how God can and will work through anything.

Then he repeats the promise. "God will surely take care of you." (Genesis 50:25)

"Surely." Really? Yes. Joseph's story shows how God is always at work behind the scenes. Claim that for your troubles, for your mistakes, for your heartaches. Claim it through the continuing frustrations and fears we are all experiencing through the global pandemic and its associated stresses. Claim it through all the injustice and unfairness. Say to all that, "You meant it for evil, but God meant it for good."

That sentence means you have a choice: to obsess on the evil or to anticipate the good. To see nothing but obstacles. Or to see opportunities. Even the agonizing wait for the pandemic to subside is a chance to serve others as Joseph did in prison.

Dave Dravecky told me that if God offered him a chance to go back in time and do it all over, he would still trade a long baseball career for a life of impact. Yet he says the biggest benefit was one he only saw clearly years later. His own character changed.

Your pain may not give you a platform for thousands or allow you to rescue your starving family. You may not see healing before heaven. But it can craft your character to become more joyful and confident and peaceful. That's God taking care of you too.

So listen to Joseph's words. Receive them in faith.

"God will surely take care of you."

God is at work, even when you don't see it. Even when you are tired of waiting for things to change. Even now.

You may worry that you missed God's Plan A for your life, because of your own mistakes or someone else's misdeeds, and now you are doomed to Plan B forever. But that's not what happened to Abraham. Or to Isaac or Jacob or Joseph. They hesitated. They deviated. They were subverted and diverted. Looked like Plan A passed them by. But God does not consign them to Plan B.

God rewrites Plan A.

Trusting that is living faith forward.

19
faith gives instead of takes

By faith Moses' parents hid him for three months after he was born, because they saw he was no ordinary child, and they were not afraid of the king's edict. By faith Moses, when he had grown up, refused to be known as the son of Pharaoh's daughter. He chose to be mistreated along with the people of God rather than to enjoy the fleeting pleasures of sin. He regarded disgrace for the sake of Christ as of greater value than the treasures of Egypt, because he was looking ahead to his reward.

(Hebrews 11:23-26)

Faith helps you see what has true value.

"Congratulations. What you have learned will bring you wealth and success. Nothing you have learned will make you happy."

That's the message Harvard MBA students heard each year from professor Clayton M. Christensen. He wrote about the final lecture he gave his classes every semester in a *Harvard Business Review* article.

Title of his lecture: "How Can I Be Sure I'll Be Happy?"

He felt an obligation after seeing many Harvard grads, "some of the smartest and most capable people on the planet, inadvertently invest for lives of hollow unhappiness… their troubles relate right back to a short-term perspective."

Christensen quotes research indicating the most satisfying long-term motivator in our lives actually isn't making money; it's the opportunity to contribute to others.

> "In the end, we will measure our lives by our contribution, not our accumulation."
> – Clayton M. Christensen

Moses had that figured out three thousand years ago.

Faith in Moses' life begins when he's too young to know what is going on: the faith of his parents. Pharoah commands every male Hebrew child be thrown in to the Nile, but they hide Moses until he's found and adopted by Pharoah's own daughter.

Then at about 40, Moses suddenly chooses to leave his gilded palace and identify with the oppressed people. He sees Egyptian wealth as "fleeting" and trades it for something of "greater value."

That's the thing with pleasures and treasures. They're not necessarily wrong. They just don't last. The new car smell, new clothes feel, new job rush, all fade. Fleeting.

Same with the world's approval. You will never catch up to what the world says you need to be. As soon as you get there it changes. It's fleeting.

Moses is just doing the math here: Following God is difficult. But really, following the world is difficult too, in the long run. So the question is, which has greater value?

Faith knows joy comes from giving, not taking.
Helping, not hoarding.
Giving, not taking.

Seems we're wired for this: A Gallup World Poll found that those who had given money away to a cause, church, or charity the previous month had higher life satisfaction.

That's why Moses' journey is recommended to you and me:

> "Command those who are rich in this present world not to be arrogant nor to put their hope in wealth, which is so uncertain, but to put their hope in God, who richly provides us with everything for our enjoyment. Command them to do good, to be rich in good deeds, and to be generous and willing to share. In this way they will lay up treasure for themselves as a firm foundation for the coming age... (1 Timothy 6:17-19)

Prosperity is a blessing. But it's easy to move from treating wealth as *God's blessing* to treating wealth *as a god*. All the things God wants me to trust him for—peace, security, fulfillment—I begin to trust pleasures and treasures to provide.

To avoid that idolatry, identify with the poor, as Moses did. It's a core biblical value for people of faith:

> "Loose the chains of injustice
> and untie the cords of the yoke,
> set the oppressed free
> and break every yoke...
> ...share your food with the hungry
> and provide the poor wanderer with shelter."
> (Isaiah 58:6,7)

Look around. Is there someone in your neighborhood you can serve, or a ministry at your church you can help?

Help others. Hope in God. That's lasting value. That's living faith forward.

20
beyond the excuses

By faith Moses left Egypt, not fearing the king's anger; he persevered because he saw him who is invisible.

(Hebrews 11:27)

Faith is trusting God more than you fear the circumstances.

Hebrews paints Moses as quite remarkable. But his journey to hero had a detour through zero.

Yes, Moses left Pharoah's palace to identify with the Hebrew slaves. But then he made a common mistake. He tried to do the right thing the wrong way. He used man's anger to enforce God's righteousness. Scripture warns that never works.

> "The anger of man does not produce the righteousness of God." (James 1:20 ESV)

Moses sees an Egyptian whipping a slave—and murders him. Then he starts telling the Hebrews what to do, and is soundly rejected. "Who set you up as boss over us? Are you going to kill us like you killed that Egyptian?" a slave asks. Disillusioned and endangered, Moses flees to the desert, where he lives in hiding for the next 40 years.

But God finds him. In Exodus chapter 3, in the desert, when Moses is an 80-year old regret-filled has-been, God's voice roars through a burning bush:

> "Go. I am sending you to Pharaoh to bring my people the Israelites out of Egypt."

And Moses is like, been there, done that, didn't work, not going back. No.

He gives God a list of excuses that sound very familiar.

Because these are my excuses. And God gives him answers that sound familiar too. Because these are promises repeated later in the Bible for all of us.

Excuse #1: I'm a nobody

> "But Moses said to God, 'Who am I that I should go to Pharaoh...?'" (Exodus 3:11a)

I relate! Many times I have thought, who am I to serve God, I know how flawed I am.

God's answer: I will be with you

> "And God said, 'I will be with you.'" (Exodus 3:12a)

Jesus says this to you too:

> "Surely I am with you always, to the very end of the age." (Matthew 28:20)

Excuse #2: I don't know what to say

> "Moses said to God, 'Suppose I go to the Israelites and say to them, 'The God of your fathers has sent me to you,' and they ask me, 'What is his name?' Then what shall I tell them?'" (Exodus 3:13)

God gives him an awesome answer. He tells him his name: "I am who I am." Then three times he uses the phrase, "Tell them this...the LORD has sent me to you."

God's answer: Tell them exactly what you've experienced!

This is God's answer to you, too. Tell them about the God *you* met and the peace *you* experience and the prayers *you've* seen answered! As the apostles said,

> "We proclaim to you what we have seen and heard..."
> (1 John 1:3a; see Acts 4:20, 22:15)

Excuse #3: What if they don't believe me?

> "What if they do not believe me or listen to me and say, 'The Lord did not appear to you'?" (Exodus 4:1)

Look at those words "what if." Obsessing on the *what ifs* can paralyze your faith.

God's answer: I will give you power!

God shows Moses three miraculous signs and says, you can do these so that they may believe that I sent you. And again, there is a parallel for you and me in the New Testament:

> "(Jesus said) But you will receive power when the Holy Spirit comes on you; and you will be my witnesses..."
> (Acts 1:8)

So God will perform fantastic miracles every single time you share your faith? No. He will give you all the power you need to do the job.

Excuse #4: I don't speak well

"Moses said to the Lord, 'O Lord, I have never been eloquent, neither in the past nor since you have spoken to your servant. I am slow of speech and tongue...Please send someone else to do it!'" (Exodus 4:10,13)

The ancient rabbis taught that Moses had a stutter. Really, the bottom line for Moses was, he just didn't want to go. This assignment was way out of his comfort zone.

God's answer: I'll send help.

In fact, he tells Moses, his brother Aaron is already on his way. God had an Aaron for Moses. And God has people for too. In fact, he is already setting them into motion. People you don't even know, people you will only meet once you step out in faith. People who could help you in your sobriety—if you step out in faith and go to that first recovery meeting. People who could help you in your walk of faith— once you join a small group. People who will be lifelong allies—once you become part of that volunteer team.

Like Moses...
You have God's presence.
You have your testimony.
You have His power.
You are part of a team.
What are you waiting for?

Remember, **nothing ever happens to people who always say no.** Say yes to God and see what miracles happen! That is living faith forward.

21
faith in what God has done

By faith he kept the Passover and the application of blood, so that the destroyer of the firstborn would not touch the firstborn of Israel.

(Hebrews 11:28)

Faith is simply confidence in the trustworthiness of God.

First Moses tries diplomacy.
Pharoah just laughs.

Moses tries a few miracles.
Pharoah is unimpressed.

Then God sends plagues.
After each one Pharoah digs in deeper.

Finally, for the terrible last plague, all the first-born sons will die—an echo of how it all started when Pharoah commanded the first-born sons of the Hebrews slaves be killed.

But God provides a way out of even this terrible calamity.

Passover.

The Hebrew families hold one last supper in their Egyptian homes. Lamb dinner. They are told to take the lamb's blood and daub it on their doors. The angel of death will "pass over" those houses, sparing them.

This is not only for the Hebrew slaves. The Book of Exodus tells us there were Egyptians among the people of God that night too. Anyone who accepted God's provision was saved. No matter who they were.

I imagine some were full of faith as they put that blood on their doorposts, absolutely confident in God's deliverance, while others thought, "OK, this is weird, but what do I have to lose?" Whether their faith was big or small, they were saved by the blood of that lamb.

Fast forward about a thousand years.

When Jesus has the Last Supper with his disciples the night before his crucifixion, it is a Passover meal. Jesus uses elements of it to teach about his impending death.

Then Jesus is referred to as the Passover lamb in the New Testament. The Apostle Paul wrote,

> "For Christ, our Passover lamb, has been sacrificed."
> (1 Corinthians 5:7b).

See the point? If we trust in his provision, bought with his blood on the cross, we are forgiven. We move from death to life. Some hear that and are full of faith. Others think, "Ok, well, I don't totally get it, but what do I have to lose?" Both are equally saved by the blood of the lamb.

As Tim Keller points out, "You are not saved by the *quality* of your faith. You are saved because of the *object* of your faith – the redeemer."

> "For it is by grace you have been saved, through faith—and this is not from yourselves, it is the gift of God— not by works, so that no one can boast." (Ephesians 2:8,9)

Remember, the first-century readers of Hebrews are being tempted to abandon the little Christian movement, with its key concept of peace with God by grace through faith, and return to a religion of works—something with sacrifices and spectacle and priests and temples. The author is arguing in Hebrews, that doesn't work, and that has never worked.

"Day after day every priest stands and performs his religious duties; again and again he offers the same sacrifices, which can never take away sins." (Hebrews 10:11)

From antiquity, true faith was never about that. It was simpler than that. Humans have ever only been able to connect to God by faith.

This continuity is especially important for the early Christians of Jewish background (and that was most) to understand. The author is reassuring them that Christianity is not a break with their faith, it is a continuation and completion of their faith, of what their forefathers all practiced. The new covenant of Jesus is the logical fulfillment of these core ideas: God exists, God is good, God rewards, God provides. God showed all that to be true in the ultimate way through Christ's perfect sacrifice for all humanity:

"Christ has appeared once for all at the culmination of the ages to do away with sin by the sacrifice of himself." (Hebrews 9:26b)

From Abel's sacrifice to Abraham's trust to Moses' Passover to Jesus' sacrifice, the revelation has grown but the relationship is the same: Simple faith in God's provision.

That is living faith forward.

22
faith says
thank you

By faith the people passed through the Red Sea as on dry land; but when the Egyptians tried to do so, they were drowned.

(Hebrews 11:29)

Faith fuels gratitude.
Gratitude fuels faith.

Moses has come a long way.
In the desert he raised objections in fear.
On the Red Sea shore he raises his staff in faith.

Sea splits. Israelites walk. Egyptians pursue. Moses raises
his staff again and the sea surges back, sweeping away the
soldiers and saving the slaves' lives.

Then he stops to write a song.

Moses, the Bible says, was "educated in all the learning of
the Egyptians," which must have included the arts. He knows
music is the best way to remember something, and hopes
the people never forget this.

They had no weapons. They faced the world's best army.
They were doomed. God came through.

After each verse, dancing women repeat the chorus:

> "I will sing to the LORD,
> for he is highly exalted.
> The horse and the rider
> he has hurled into the sea." (Exodus 15:1,21)

Look at some of the verses. What words do you see
repeated?

> "Your right hand, LORD,
> was majestic in power.
> Your right hand, LORD,

shattered the enemy.
You stretch out your right hand,
and the earth swallows your enemies." (Exodus 15:6,12)

Wait. Whose arm and whose right hand held the staff that split the sea? Moses'. His arm, his hand, his staff, in clear view of a million refugees.

Yet in this moment when the slightest self-promotion could have sealed him as sole dictator, he says:

Look what God did.

Yeah, Moses has come a long way. Whose arm struck down that Egyptian oppressor 40 years earlier? Moses'. He had set out to be The Great Hebrew Deliverer. By his own right hand. Now he sings a different tune.

God's name is mentioned 13 times in this song. Plus 33 pronouns. 46 total references to God. Moses' name does not appear once.

Look who has the "I" problem:

"The enemy boasted,
'I will pursue
I will overtake
I will divide…
I will gorge…
I will draw my sword
My hand will destroy.
But you blew a breath,
and the sea covered them." (Exodus 15:9,10)

A puff of God's breath and man's puffed-up ego is popped.

Moses knows it's not about him. It's all about God. The song he sings is an utter repudiation of the cult-like authoritarian leadership in many churches and countries, and a stunning contrast to our celebrity-driven, self-promoting culture.

It's tough because we all need to make a living and in a very noisy world full of a trillion posts on a billion screens you feel the need to stand out just to get work. Seems part of modern life is to use every chance for self-promotion.

Real experts at this have perfected the "humblebrag," a boast disguised as humility. Today Moses might be tempted to post a selfie: "Embarrassed by my old shepherd's staff while parting the Red Sea today."

God knows you need work and worth. He knows you need to have a sense of achievement and success.

But remember to keep perspective. Without God, you would be nothing.

Little self-inventory:
How often do I use the words "I" and "me" in conversations?
How often do I use the words "thank you"?

Focusing on the One who gave me everything. That's living faith forward.

23
when faith hits a wall

By faith the walls of Jericho fell, after the army had marched around them for seven days.

(Hebrews 11:30)

Faith trusts that my future tense is God's past tense.

I ran track and cross-country in high school, and have continued running as a hobby after that, mostly 10Ks and half-marathons. I'm far from expert, but I've run enough to know this: the hardest part of a long-distance race is not starting. That part's easy. The hardest part is not even finishing. When I see that finish line I always get a burst of energy for a final kick.

The hardest part is when you hit what every runner dreads, what every runner has experienced. The Wall.

You can't see it. But you sure feel it.

The Wall is the part of the race, about two-thirds of the way through, when it feels like you can't take another step. Every muscle screams for you to stop. Your lungs are burning, your feet are sore, your mind is fatigued. So a huge part of race training is psychological. What do you do when you hit The Wall?

Maybe you're there right now. You hit the wall in a relationship. In a ministry. Maybe in your faith. You just want to quit. Remember, the original readers of Hebrews were there too.

So I love the next story in Hebrews 11 because it is *literally* about hitting a wall. A huge city wall.

Moses led the Israelites right up to the Jordan River, the border of the Promised Land, Now he has died, and his successor Joshua and the Israelites have to get past Jericho, a walled fortress city that was like a castle guarding passage into the land.

> "Now the gates of Jericho were securely barred because of the Israelites. No one went out and no one came in. Then the Lord said to Joshua, "See, I have delivered Jericho into your hands..." (Joshua 6:1,2)

Notice how the Lord said, "I have delivered." Past tense. But Joshua looks up and what does he see? "The gates of Jericho securely barred..." God is speaking in the *past tense* about a battle that Joshua *has not yet fought yet*.

Throughout Scripture God does the same thing for you and me. He speaks in the *past tense* about battles you are *currently fighting*.

> "Those he predestined he also called, those he called he also justified, those he justified he also glorified." (Romans 8:30)

"Wait," you may be thinking. "I know I have been called and justified, but I have not been glorified yet. That happens in heaven."

God is speaking in past tense about what is yet to come.

He has seen your future.
He knows his grace will be sufficient for you.
He knows you will be perfected into Christlikeness.
He knows you will be glorified.

Does that mean you will never go through tough times?
Of course not.
It means you're going to be ok.
It means you have a destiny that is assured.
It means you can move forward confidently.

Even when it seems to take forever.

24
faith doesn't stop on six

Let us not become weary in doing good, for at the proper time we will reap a harvest if we do not give up.

(Galatians 6:9)

**Daily obedience is my responsibility.
Ultimate outcome is God's responsibility.**

The Silicon Valley, where I grew up, used to be more like Apricot Valley. It was where most of the apricots in the world were grown commercially.

One thing that makes truly fresh, sun-ripened apricots so precious: harvest only lasts about a week or two, right around the Fourth of July. All that work, for one whole year, no payoff, then suddenly, they're all ripe. And it's not like you get a preview apricot every month just to keep you motivated.

You get *nothing*. Until—you get *everything*.

Joshua is told to march his army around the city for six days. Only on the seventh would the results suddenly come: the wall would fall. They didn't get a preview brick. Not even a little crumbling mortar. Imagine how those soldiers felt: "What is happening? How long's this gonna take? I am walking and it is NOT WORKING."

You may feel exactly the same way. It feels like you've marched and marched for days. Years. And not one brick has dropped. But sometimes you see nothing until the breakthrough moment. Then suddenly it all happens.

As I heard another pastor say, "Don't stop on six!" What if the wall is doomed on day seven?

When I hit The Wall while running, I would tell myself, "I am not quitting now. I will run until I reach that next telephone pole... or that next street corner... or that sign." When I reached that marker, I found I had strength to go a little further. Until finally the race was done.

Same thing with the walls I hit now. Researchers say 60% of pastors want to quit. The stresses of the last year and a half feel like The Wall. I tell my friends in ministry (and myself), "Just don't quit now. Tell yourself you plan to quit in two years." To be honest, I have lasted 28 years at the church I serve in two-year increments—from day one! I took the job thinking I would be the unintentional two-year interim pastor, and I'm still here 28 years later.

March for one more day.
Because you never know.
That wall might fall tomorrow.

Harvest will come.
Walls will fall.
Keep doing what God asked you to do.

One step at a time.
One day at a time.
One lap at a time.

Do you see how that's a characteristic of every single story in Hebrews 11?

Daily obedience is my responsibility.
Ultimate outcome is God's responsibility.

That is living faith forward.

25
faith changes destinies

By faith the prostitute Rahab, because she welcomed the spies, was not killed with those who were disobedient.

(Hebrews 11:31)

Your mess can be part of your message.

Did you notice it?

The author to the Hebrews only alludes to Joshua without ever mentioning his name, but really spotlights Rahab. In fact she's the only character from Israel's conquest of the Promised Land mentioned by name. And not only her name. Also her...uh...profession.

Why do you think the author specifies Rahab was a prostitute? Why not leave that out? Many have tried. Josephus, a first century Jewish historian, changed her profession to "innkeeper" when he retold the story to his Roman audience.

So why is it listed here? Let's look at her story.

Joshua sends spies into the city of Jericho. When they get there, they need to hide, so they find a place where it wouldn't seem too odd to observe men sneaking around with faces covered by hoods: a house of prostitution.

But apparently they were terrible spies, because almost instantly the King of Jericho finds out and dispatches men to Rahab's house. She sends the king's agents on a wild goose chase. Then she makes a deal with the spies.

> "I know the Lord has given you this land," she told them... "For the Lord your God is the supreme God of the heavens above and the earth below. Now swear to me by the Lord that you will be kind to me and my family since I have helped you. Give me some guarantee that

when Jericho is conquered, you will let me live, along with my father and mother, my brothers and sisters, and all their families." (Joshua 2:9–13)

Rahab's story shows me three principles:

• Your salvation depends on grace

Rahab is no innocent. She is a prostitute. Not only is she a prostitute; she is a Canaanite prostitute. Not only is she a Canaanite prostitute; she lives in Jericho, the citadel of the enemy. Rahab's only hope is to receive mercy. Same with you and me.

> "A salvation earned by good works and moral effort would favor the more able, competent, accomplished, and privileged. But salvation by sheer grace favors the failed, the outsiders, the weak, because it goes only to those who know salvation *must* be by sheer grace... Thus the Bible does not show us story after story of 'heroes of the faith' who go from strength to strength. Instead we get a series of narratives containing figures who are usually not the people the world would expect to be spiritual paragons and leaders." – Tim Keller

• Your history doesn't determine your destiny

Rahab was brought into the family. I mean, *really* brought into the family. She becomes the great-grandmother of King David. And then, in the first pages of the New Testament, there's a great reveal. Rahab is the great-great-great (times a few greats) grandmother of... wait for it.. *Jesus!*

She serves as an icon for the radical inclusiveness of God's grace for anyone who receives it. Take a closer look at the cast of characters associated with the events of Hebrews 11 and you'll see an astonishingly diverse group. Moses' wife Zipporah was a black African, not an Israelite (Numbers 12). Both late-bloomer Enoch and tent-peg-warrior Jael, the woman who killed the evil Sisera, were descendants of Cain, not Abel (Genesis 5, Judges 4). Joshua's fellow spy Caleb was a descendant of Esau, not Jacob (Numbers 14). Rahab was descended from Ham, from whom the Canaanites and several African kingdoms also traced their lineage (Joshua 2). The point is, none were part of God's covenant with Abraham by *birth*. But they were included by *faith*.

Maybe you have felt excluded from some group because of your own ethnic heritage or personal history. As you pass the elite cliques you hear whispers of judgement. Or you hear those whispers from your own conscience—whispers of condemnation because of choices you now regret. You wonder if you belong, if God really has a plan for you. Rahab's story is your story. She shows God liberating and welcoming someone just like you.

• **Your mess can be part of your message**

In fact, God can redeem your past, use your history as part of your ministry. Rahab has inspired many who felt they were just too bad for God.

When I worked at a Christian radio station in Nevada we would get phone calls at times from prostitutes who worked at brothels nearby. They asked for prayer. Had questions about the Bible. Requested hymns. We tried to connect them with a ministry to prostitutes there. Why did they call a Christian station? As one told me in tears, "I know Jesus loved people like me."

Somehow she had heard about Jesus welcoming prostitutes, viewing them differently than anyone else. Why do you suppose he did? Maybe, just maybe, he was thinking of great-great-great-great grandma.

26
in your father's eyes

And what more shall I say? I do not have time to tell about Gideon…

(Hebrews 11:32)

Faith listens to what God is saying to me... about me.

Ever feel you have zero to offer God? No amazing talents or skills, no astounding courage or faith, and in fact, you're not even sure you believe all this stuff?

Meet Gideon.

When he first appears in the Bible, he's hiding in a hole.

Bad guys called the Midianites are ravaging the land, and Gideon has no intention of fighting them off. He just wants to bake some bread.

> "Gideon was threshing wheat in a winepress to keep it from the Midianites." (Judges 6:11b)

Wheat in a winepress? What's that about?

To thresh grain, you take a pile of it, put it in a basket, toss it into the air. The heavy grain falls back into the basket, the lighter chaff blows away. You toss it over and over until nothing is left but the good stuff. Usually you do this where it's breezy. In the open. On a hilltop.

Problem is, the Midianites would watch. And if they saw little clouds of chaff they knew, "Someone's got grain!" And they'd ride out and steal it.

So Gideon is hiding in a wine press. A big hole in the ground. If he's threshing grain down there, he's choking on the dust. Once in a while his head pokes up to gasp for air and check for bad guys.

(Cough, cough) "Any Midianites?" Down like a gopher.

(Wheeze, cough) "Now? Nope." Back into the hole.

Until one time he pops his head up and— "Wha--?!"— sees an angel sitting under an oak tree. Hey, he wasn't there a minute ago. Watch what happens next:

> "When the angel of the Lord appeared to Gideon, he said, 'The Lord is with you, mighty warrior."
> Judges 6:12)

I love the way some other translations try to capture this Hebrew phrase:

> "Mighty man of valor!" (NKJV)

> "You mighty man of fearless courage!" (Amplified)

Wait. He is hiding in a hole in the ground. Poking his head up like a scared rabbit. Yet the angel of God looks at this ancient version of Barney Fife and says, "Hello, you mighty man of fearless courage!"

God does not see you for what you are.
God sees you for what you can be.

Like in the Book of Acts. Ananias is told by God to go heal a man named Saul. Ananias objects, "Lord, are you kidding? That's the guy who's been dragging Christians like me off to prison!"

God replies, "This is my chosen vessel who will take the gospel to kings."

We see ourselves in terms of yesterday and today.
God sees us in terms of tomorrow and forever.

So, you may ask, "How does God see *me*?" Great question.

> "He chose us in him before the creation of the world to be holy and blameless in his sight." (Ephesians 1:4)

> "See what great love the Father has lavished on us, that we should be called children of God!" (1 John 3:1a)

> "You are a chosen people, a royal priesthood, a holy nation, God's special possession," (1 Peter 2:9)

Chosen. Holy. Blameless. God's child. God's treasure. God's priest.

Sound too good to be true? Probably exactly what it sounded like to the coward hiding in a hole.

Faith doesn't start with our faith in God. It starts with God speaking words of faith to us.

Are you listening to what he is saying, you powerful person of inspiring courage?

27
faith words

Do not let any unwholesome talk come out of your mouths, but only what is helpful for building others up...

(Ephesians 4:29)

By my words I can build faith up or tear it down.

Are you speaking as God's angel spoke to Gideon?
Or are you the voice of another, fallen angel?

Ask yourself this simple question:
"What sort of things am I consistently saying to others —
and to myself?"

You mighty person of valor.
Or
You weak person of probable failure.

The tongue, the Bible says, is like the rudder of a ship. It's small, but it sets the course of your life (James 3:4,5). By your words you can set yourself up for failure. You can set your children up for failure. Your church. Your country. Your relationships.

"I feel sorry for you kids, this world you're growing up in."
"Nothing good will ever come out of Washington."
"Churches in America are going downhill fast."

Rudders that steer the ship.

> "By our speech we can ruin the world, turn harmony to chaos, throw mud on a reputation, send the whole world up in smoke and go up in smoke with it, smoke right from the pit of hell." (James 3:5 The Message)

Here's another way to put it that ties into Hebrews 11: What is your **meta-narrative**– the way you narrate your life? What is the big picture you have about where history is going?

What are you saying to yourself about yourself? That's your rudder.

God has a plan for you.
God will empower you.
God is working in you and through you.

Or

This will probably never work.
You're not capable.
You're such a failure.

You are setting a course either way.

I will never forget when I was very young, feeling very worried about the future after the death of my father, my Swiss-Italian Aunt Pia cupped my chin in her hands and looked me in the eyes and pronounced, "You are something special, Rene! I cannot wait to see how God uses you!" She said that to me when I was four. I still remember it. Yeah. Words change people.

I am not saying just be positive, don't grieve, don't lament, don't critique. Grieving and lamenting and critiquing are actually very productive. I'm talking about eliminating speech where you indulge the worst side of your nature. Complaining speech. Grumbling speech. Critical speech.

One of my biggest concerns about Christians right now: How much we're influenced by our society's way of communicating. Seems every talk show host, every podcaster, every social media influencer, whether conservative or liberal or Christian or anything else, is all about controversy. Picking fights. Finding fault. Being critical. All the time. About every little thing.

But Ephesians 4:29 says,

> "Do not let any unwholesome talk come out of your mouths, but only what is helpful for building others up according to their needs, that it may benefit those who listen."

There are Gideons all around you today, hiding in holes, afraid of the bad guys. They poke their heads up once in a while. There. Did you see them? That weak hello. That tentative email. The nervous text.

Look for ways to be their angel. Help them see themselves as the mighty men and women God created them to be.

Help them live faith forward.

28
faith even for the weirdos

...Barak, Samson, Jephthah...who through faith conquered kingdoms, administered justice, and gained what was promised.

(Hebrews 11:32,33)

Faith is believing God can use anyone.

Some of the people in Hebrews 11 did things that could get them arrested today. Is that hard for you to accept?

When I pastored a church at South Lake Tahoe I was inspired by an attorney in town named Kenny. I visited jail inmates with Kenny many times. Kenny was a criminal attorney so he saw them with clarity. He knew exactly what they had done. The pain they had caused. That they were not all nice people.

Yet Kenny loved them. Because he believed God loved them. Once someone asked me, "Why do you and Kenny waste time with all those warped weirdos?"

I didn't know what to say. I invited him to jail, but he never joined us. Now I think I would first invite him on a walk through Hebrews 11. More than a few "warped weirdos" in here.

You've met a prostitute, a polygamist, several cowards, and a hedonist. Now, three more for that colorful list. The author is really reaching down deep into the history bag for these characters.

The date: Over 3,000 years ago.
The Late Bronze Age Collapse.
For reasons still not fully understood, around 1,200 B.C. all the Mediterranean societies collapsed into chaos. It's Conan the Barbarian time.

That's where these three guys come in.

Barak. The Israelites suffer under the oppressive Canaanite king Jabin and his cruel general Sisera. Their nine hundred iron chariots rumble menacingly through the land.

A wise woman named Deborah leads Israel at the time. She tells Barak God has chosen him to recruit ten thousand men to fight Sisera. Barak says he's not so sure.

> "If you go with me, I will go. But if you don't go with me, I won't go." (Judges 4:8 NLT)

Deborah sees this not so much as a vote of confidence in her leadership than an attempt to weasel out of battle. She says, OK, but, "Because of the way you are going about this, the honor will not be yours, for the Lord will hand Sisera over to a woman."

Nine hundred Canaanite chariots are no match for ten thousand Israelite guerillas. Sisera abandons his chariot to hide in the tent of an ally. Then that man's wife, Jael, drives a tent peg through his head with a hammer while he is sleeping. Whoa.

The people are freed. And Deborah writes a song with *seven verses* about how Jael… uh… made her point. Barak? Sort of an afterthought.

Samson. An angel tells an infertile woman she will bear a Chosen Child, anointed by God to free his people. And what does this Chosen Child do? Frivolous feats and amorous misadventures. Kills a thousand Philistines with a bone. Sleeps with a prostitute. Falls in love with a spy. And here's the thing: Nothing he does actually helps. Twenty years of muscle-flexing and it's all still chaos.

Only at the end of his life does Samson seem to come to his senses. He brings down Philistine HQ with one last burst of power.

OK...

Jephthah. The worst.

One time he goes to battle and vows to God, "If I am victorious, whatever comes out of my house when I return will be sacrificed to the Lord." He wins. He returns. His daughter runs out to greet him. And foolishly he fulfills his vow.

Nope. Don't get it. Why is his name on this list?

Jephthah is recognized for his best moments. Not the madness into which he descended. His mother was a prostitute. His brothers hate him. The village elders drive him out. Yet he is so successful in protecting his people that they make him their leader. And unlike almost any of the other warriors during the period of the Judges, his first instinct is always diplomacy. He tries to be a man of peace. Until that one time.

Three flawed people. Like, *extremely* flawed. What's the takeaway?

I hope you are not inspired to gleefully screw up.
I hope you are inspired to joyfully have hope.
All their missteps caused a ton of pain.

But God in his grace still loves them.

In fact Jesus looks at all these incomprehensibly inconsistent people and makes a surprising declaration. It's in a beautiful passage earlier in Hebrews.

> "Jesus is not ashamed to call them brothers and sisters. He says, 'I will declare your name to my brothers and sisters; in the assembly I will sing your praises…' And again he says, "Here am I, and the children God has given me." (Hebrews 2:11b-13)

The astonishing thing about our Lord is that he feels the same way about all the warped and wounded and weird people as he does about… you.

Better embrace that.

Because, truth be told, we are all more warped and wounded and weird than we may care to admit—or even see.

Read these stories for hope. As Max Lucado points out, "A surprising and welcome discovery of the Bible is this: God uses failures. Though you failed, God's love does not. So face your failures with faith in God's goodness."

That is living faith forward.

29
the root
of faith

I do not have time to tell about ... David and Samuel and the prophets...

(Hebrews 11:32b)

Faith hears God whisper, "I choose you."

The mysterious prophet Samuel visits Bethlehem one night on a secret mission: King Saul is insane and must be replaced. Samuel commands Jesse, "Bring all your sons before me." One of them is about to be chosen king.

Samuel must have been imagining the sort of person God would select. Saul is described in Scripture as tall and powerful. So Samuel's probably picturing someone who can out-tall and out-power Saul. A younger upgrade, Saul 2.0.

Samuel looks up at the strapping oldest son, Eliab, and thinks, "This must be God's choice." God says no.

So Samuel passes on son number one. And the next. And the next, and the next, and the next, and the next, all the way down the line, until he runs out of candidates. Finally Samuel asks Jesse, "Are these all the sons you have?" Jesse's answer is very telling. Well…

> "There is still the youngest, but he is out in the fields watching the sheep and goats." (1 Samuel 16:11 NLT)

I'm not the first to wonder why you'd leave one of your sons with the goats when a famed kingmaker asks to see them all.

And notice how Jesse doesn't even call David by name. He just says, "the youngest." In Hebrew, the word is *haqqaton*. It can mean "the baby." Some suggest it even implies "the runt." The same word was used for a pinky finger. *Haqqaton*. "Well, there's pinky."

And of course it turns out—David's the one. God chooses the family runt. When David finally arrives, God tells Samuel:

"Rise and anoint him; he is the one." (1 Samuel 16:12b)

I've heard a lot of preachers do a lot of guesswork about the reasons God must have chosen David. He had proven himself loyal by tending sheep. Shown himself brave by defeating lions. Demonstrated devotion by composing psalms.

Problem is, none of that is in the text.

This story is not about how David somehow *earned* God's blessing. The point is that God simply *picked* him. When no one else did.

You've seen God do that all through Hebrews 11. *Hey, Abraham. Sarah. Moses. Gideon. I choose you.*

He says it to you too.

A thousand years after David, the Apostle Paul wrote these words to a Corinthian church full of people least likely to be selected for any kind of honor:

"Few of you were wise in the world's eyes or powerful or wealthy when God called you. But God chose the foolish things of the world to shame the wise; God chose the weak things of the world to shame the strong…"
(1 Corinthians 1:26b-27)

As Brennan Manning puts it:

> "Grace calls out, 'You are not just a disillusioned old man who may die soon, a middle-aged woman stuck in a job and desperately wanting to get out, a young person feeling the fire in the belly begin to grow cold. You may be insecure, inadequate, mistaken or potbellied. Death, panic, depression, and disillusionment may be near you. But you are not just that. You are accepted.' Never confuse your perception of yourself with the mystery that you really are accepted."

It is all a gift. Even the faith to believe in this grace is a gift. Here's why it is so important for you to lean into that. Although David is chosen, he does not coast into the kingdom. Between here and there, he will face battles and betrayals, slipups and successes, fans and assassins. How does he get through it?

He continually directs his thoughts back to *this moment*.

This is precisely the point for the original readers of Hebrews.

Your chosenness does not mean life will be struggle-free. So remember, you have a destiny. You are beloved by God. Called.

That's important to remember.

Because there are giants up ahead.

30
reframing
in faith

The Lord who delivered me from the paw of
the lion and the paw of the bear will deliver
me from the hand of this Philistine.

(1 Samuel 17:37 NIV)

Trusting God with your future is about seeing Him work in your past.

You know the story. For 40 days, every day and every night, a giant of a man comes out to the field and shouts, "Choose a man to fight me! I defy the armies of Israel!"

And what's the response from the Israelite army? Every day, when the Israelites saw the man, "they all ran from him in great fear." (1 Samuel 17:24)

They didn't fight. They didn't go home either. They just did the same ineffective thing. Every single day. *For 40 days.* That's what fear does. It leads to a paralysis of the will. You're mesmerized by the problem constantly, aware enough to stay worried, too afraid to act.

Finally somebody does something. A teenager accepts the challenge.

A less-than-careful retelling of this story can sell it short. The way it's often taught sounds like *The Little Shepherd That Could*: David defeated a giant because he kept saying, "I think I can, I think I can." And though you may feel small, if you have faith in yourself, then you can do it too!

Not quite the message here.

Watch what David tells King Saul:

> "I have been taking care of my father's sheep and goats," he said. "When a lion or a bear comes to steal a lamb from the flock, I go after it with a club and rescue

the lamb from its mouth… I have done this to both lions and bears, and I'll do it to this pagan Philistine, too…" (1 Samuel 17:34-36 NLT)

What's funny to me is that I would've seen all this as a string of bad luck: "A lion attacked. And a bear attacked. And another lion and another bear. And now a giant! What am I, a magnet for trouble?" Not David.

"The Lord who delivered me from the paw of the lion and the paw of the bear will deliver me from the hand of this Philistine." (1 Samuel 17:37)

Tania Luna, psychologist and author of a study published in *Child Psychology and Psychiatry*, says reframing negative experiences can help you lessen trauma, boost optimism, and increase resilience.

For one study she showed kids intense images, like a dog growling, while measuring their brain activity. Then she had them look at the same images again, but this time with comforting explanations, like: "This dog is defending a little girl." Their brain scans showed a sharp drop in activity in the region of the brain that processes fear. "It was like they were seeing completely different photos," Luna says.

She says adults who are able to get past setbacks process them similarly. They don't deny the traumatic event, but they add personal narration that redeems the picture: "I grew. I learned. I deepened. I am a better person now."

David does something similar with his own photo gallery of growling bears and roaring lions. He reframes their attacks.

He sees God developing him for this very moment.

My sister and I both feel our childhood traumas, starting with our father's death when we were both toddlers and continuing through years of poverty and other setbacks, deepened us into people we would not have become without those difficulties. We gained a mature perspective on the value of life and faith and family at a very young age. The pain was real, yet it brought with it wisdom and empathy. Reframing our own tragedies has helped us transition from grief to gratitude.

Trusting God with your *future* is about remembering how He worked in your *past*. Because you can't see the future. No matter how hard you try. That's what drives you crazy sometimes. But you *can* see the *past*.

So think of a past trial.
Consider how God redeemed the pain, answered prayer, provided assistance, sent a friend, gave you grace, healed your heart grew you, stretched you, blessed you, saved you.

The lions and bears were real.
They were fierce.
But so was God's presence and power.

That means he can help you fight even the giant shouting at you today.

31
action
breeds faith

David ran quickly toward the battle line to meet him.

(1 Samuel 17:48 NIV)

Faith thrives on movement.

So now the tension is really mounting. David and Goliath have made their speeches. They approach each other on the battlefield.

And David does what no one has dared for 40 days.

> "As the Philistine moved closer to attack him, David ran quickly toward the battle line to meet him."
> (1 Samuel 17:48 NIV)

Ran quickly.

After all is said and done, you have to stop just sitting there thinking about it, and start running to meet the challenge. You can get paralysis by analysis. At some point you just need to *act*. Like David did.

Action breeds courage. Tennyson wrote, "I must lose myself in action, lest I wither in despair." David lost himself in action while the rest of the army had been withering in despair for forty days.

Have you noticed this is a theme of Hebrews 11? Faith moves ahead. Abraham, Joshua, Gideon, all advanced into the unknown. Some more confidently than others. But forward they went.

As David sprints toward Goliath, the cacophony in the valley is stilled. Two armies hold their collective breath.

They hear Goliath's armor clanking.

David's sling spinning.
The stone whistling.
Smack.
The End.

40 days of stalling, 40 days of worrying, 40 days of anxiety, and the match lasts maybe two minutes.
Goliath falls like a sack of rocks.
It's over. Days of delay—and a few moments of action solve the problem.

It can happen for you too.

Run to battle. Do something. Turn to action instead of despair.

What happens if you just keep doing nothing?
Your anxiety intensifies.
You lose another hour of sleep.
You delay any progress.

What happens if you do something?
You'll probably make some progress.
You may just slay that giant.

Maybe you feel that all you have is a pebble's worth of potential versus a Goliath-sized problem. But so what? If God is involved, who knows what you're setting into motion?

Put your pebble into play. And see what happens next.

That's living faith forward.

32
faith stays standing

...the prophets, who through faith conquered kingdoms, administered justice, and gained what was promised; who shut the mouths of lions, quenched the fury of the flames, and escaped the edge of the sword.

(Hebrews 11:33,34)

Faith is living by conviction instead of circumstance.

When Hebrews 11 mentions prophets who "quenched
the fury of the flames," there's only one place the original
readers' minds would have gone: a vast plain near ancient
Babylon where the world saw three young men stand up
while everyone else bowed down.

A massive idol looms over the valley. It's nine stories high. It's
on a stage in the desert. Thousands of the rich and famous
show up to celebrate. Picture Burning Man, only this is
Golden Man. Oh, and if you don't bow down? You will be the
burning man. In the furnace. Conveniently set up right next to
the statue. King's orders.

Alone in this vast plain, three young men, Meshach,
Shadrach, and Abednego, do not bow. They boldly explain,

> "If we are thrown into the blazing furnace, **the God we
> serve is able** to deliver us from it, and he will deliver us
> from your majesty's hand." (Daniel 3:17)

Ray Johnston says everybody operates by one of four
dominant life principles.

Circumstances: "What's happening around me?"

Convenience: "What's easiest?"

Criticism: "What will others think?"

Convictions: "What matters most?"

Everyone else in the valley that day let circumstances, convenience, and criticism push their buttons. Only these three lived by conviction.

The God we serve is able. Live by this conviction and you'll never cower.

The God we serve is able to heal wounded marriages. I've seen it happen. The God we serve is able to free people from addictions. I've watched him do it. The God we serve is able to reconcile broken relationships. I've experienced it myself.

God is able. Only one conviction is more powerful:

> "But **even if he does not**, we want you to know, your majesty, that we still will not serve your gods or worship the image of gold you have set up." (Daniel 3:18)

Can you decide to have *even if he does not* faith?

"God is able to heal me of cancer, but even if he does not—
"God is able to turn my kids around, but even if he does not—
"God is able to get me a job, but even if he does not—

"...I will still serve him."

Someone said these guys had an "I don't have to survive" attitude. If you're going to stand up for what's right, you're going to need that.

King says, OK, you won't survive then! They are thrown into the fire. Then something amazing happens.

"King Nebuchadnezzar leaped to his feet in amazement and asked his advisers, 'Weren't there three men that we tied up and threw into the fire?' They replied, 'Certainly, your majesty.'

"He said, 'Look! I see four men walking around in the fire, unbound and unharmed, and the fourth looks like a son of the gods.'" (Daniel 3:24,25)

The king is so astonished he orders them freed from the flames and they survive unscathed.

Who do you think that fourth man was? I believe it was Jesus, in a pre-incarnate appearance. And I believe that exact same fourth man is with you right now and will never leave you nor forsake you.

When you believe that to be true, you can make the switch from being driven by circumstances or conveniences or criticism to conviction.

God is able. But I will live by my convictions even if I do not see him act.

That is living faith forward.

33
faith to face
the future

...who shut the mouths of lions...

(Hebrews 11:33b)

"Every tomorrow has two handles. We can take hold of it with the handle of anxiety or the handle of faith." – Henry Ward Beecher

The writer to the Hebrews alludes to Daniel when he refers to those who "shut the mouths of lions." Classic story. Daniel refuses to worship the King. So he's thrown into the lion's den. When the lions don't eat him, he is set free. Great. But here's what I want to know: Where did Daniel's courage come from?

I think you can trace it to a time he was truly terrified.

Ever crack open parts of the Bible like the book of Revelation and get a little scared and a little confused? Or forget the Bible—ever read the daily headlines and get a little scared and confused? Well, you're in good company. In the Book of Daniel, God reveals several apocalyptic visions of the future. After the first one, Daniel says,

> "I, Daniel, was worried. The visions that went through my mind frightened me. (Daniel 7:15 NCV)

It gets worse. After an angel explains it, he says it again:

> "I, Daniel, was very afraid. My face became white from fear, but I kept everything to myself." (Daniel 7:28 NCV)

Then after the next vision:

> "I, Daniel, became very weak and was sick for several days after that vision. Then I got up and went back to work for the king, but I was very upset about the vision. I didn't understand what it meant." (Daniel 8:27 NCV)

Then a messenger from heaven is sent to Daniel to calm him down. Daniel says his body was shining, his face was like lightning, his eyes were on fire, and his voice sounded like the roar of a crowd. This does not have a calming effect. Daniel sees him—and passes out.

The angelic being touches him and says, "Daniel, stand up. God loves you very much. Listen. I have been sent with a message." Daniel says, basically, not another message!

> "I said to the one standing in front of me, 'Master, I am upset and afraid because of what I saw in the vision. I feel helpless.'" (Daniel 10:16b NCV)

Then this happens. And makes Daniel into someone who could face lions:

> "The one who looked like a man touched me again and gave me strength. He said, 'Daniel, **don't be afraid. God loves you very much. Peace be with you. Be strong now; be courageous**.'" (Daniel 10:18,19 NCV)

That is God's message to you too. Every one of those truths is repeated in the Bible for every believer.

"Don't be afraid..."

Did you know a form of the phrase "don't be afraid" is in every book of the Bible?

To Joshua he says, "Do not fear."
To Zechariah, "Do not fear."
To Mary, "Do not fear."
To Joseph, "Do not fear."

First thing Jesus says after the resurrection, "do not fear."

OK, so how can I not fear?

"God loves you very much."

The word "beloved" is used nearly 70 times in the New Testament to refer to Christians. Think of what it would do to your freak-out level if you really believed God loves you.

"Peace be with you. Be strong now; be courageous."

It's not a command: "Be strong!" The sense of this phrase is, "Receive this. Be infused with strength." As Jesus told his disciples, "My peace I leave with you."

And indeed, Daniel says,

> "When he spoke to me, I became stronger and said, 'Master, speak, since you have given me strength.'" (Daniel 10:19b)

Hopelessness about the future is rampant. It can sap your strength. It sapped Daniel's. Maybe when you started reading this you were a little shaky. Maybe a lot shaky. Hear these words from heaven again as words for you right now:

> "Don't be afraid. God loves you very much. Peace be with you. Be strong now; be courageous." (Daniel 10:19)

Trusting those truths is key to living faith forward.

34
faith focuses on the finish line

Women received back their dead, raised to life again. There were others who were tortured, refusing to be released so that they might gain an even better resurrection.

(Hebrews 11:35)

"The path to the good news is blazed by those who keep moving through the bad news."
- Carey Nieuwhof

When she was just nine years old, Marla Runyan went blind. In 2000, Marla became the first legally blind athlete to ever compete in the Olympics. Since then she has won six national championships, been a two-time Olympian, was the top American in the NYC Marathon, the Boston Marathon, the Chicago Marathon, and was the 2006 National Marathon Champion.

Did I mention she's blind?

One interviewer asked, "How can you run toward a finish line you can't see?" Her reply:

"I can't see it, but I know it's there."

Great definition of living faith forward.

Hebrews 11 ends with a list of anonymous faith heroes who seemed to receive no reward. Yes, the author says, some did see miracles—even people raised from the dead (probably thinking of Elisha raising a widow's son from the dead in 2 Kings 4).

But not most. The list that follows should put to rest any false idea that having strong faith keeps bad stuff from happening. Faith is not a magic rabbit's foot. This is a grisly list of the worst kinds of trials:

"Some faced jeers and flogging, and even chains and imprisonment. They were put to death by stoning; they were sawed in two; they were killed by the sword.

"They went about in sheepskins and goatskins, destitute, persecuted and mistreated— the world was not worthy of them. They wandered in deserts and mountains, living in caves and in holes in the ground.

"These were all commended for their faith, yet none of them received what had been promised, since **God had planned something better** for us so that only together with us would they be made perfect."
(Hebrews 11:36-40)

Some teach that people with "real" faith will never have trouble. But that is not a conclusion you could possibly reach when reading Hebrews 11. These people had their world rocked. So how did they hang in there?

They trusted God for the reward

Jesus said when I obey God in this life, even in something as small as giving a cup of cold water to something thirsty, I can count on a reward at the finish line.

They trusted God for the resurrection

The resurrection. The day everything cursed by sin and death is redeemed and restored by God. The finish line.

They trusted God for the results

Some trust and obey God and He grants spectacular results in this life. Others trust the same mighty God and He enables them to endure horrific trials. The difference is not in their faith, but in God's sovereign purpose. In the case of the people on this list, God had planned something better than a new country or a new temple. He planned a new heaven and a new earth. That takes time.

"God had planned something better."

When your hopes are not perfectly fulfilled you can claim that promise too.

Here's the point. Some people receive wonderful earthly rewards for their faith. Others don't.

Yet they are all heroes.
And they are *all rewarded* in the end.
So keep your eyes on the finish line.
Even when you cannot see it.
The race is still worth it.

Marla Runyan was interviewed in 2020 when the Boston Marathon was cancelled. She's one of the organizers. She said,

> "For all athletes right now I would say, keep in your mind that vision of the future. That's what keeps me going now, that vision of us all coming back together in person and what an amazing celebration that will be for us."

Cross out the word "athletes" and put in the word "Christians" and you've got the message of these verses.

Think of the future, the vision, the amazing celebration.

That's living faith forward.

35
three stages of the faith journey

These were all commended for their faith, yet they did not receive what was promised.

(Hebrews 11:39)

Faith is not belief without proof but trust without reservation.

Hebrews 11 seems like a kaleidoscope of characters that have little in common.

Rich and poor, princes and paupers, men and women, soldiers and poets, the very old and the very young, covering centuries of human history.

But look closely. Do you see it? Every single person mentioned here has the same three components to their faith journey:

Calling.
Acting.
Enduring.

God calls them. Chooses them, anoints them, speaks his grace to them. None of them earned it. None expected it. Most could barely believe it. But they first needed to hear this: God chose them. He gives them a new identity and new destiny.

Then they act. They move in response to God's call. They take the next step. Many respond reluctantly, some barely, none perfectly. But they act in some way in answer to God's grace and God's direction.

Then they endure. Yes, they have doubts. Sins. Hesitations. Missteps. They wrestle and argue with God at times. But in the end they persevere. Even when they don't get everything they hope for, even when things fall apart, even when people mock them. Because God keeps drawing them back to their memory of his call, to the fact that they've been chosen.

Most need to repeat these steps several times. They are reminded of the call. They respond with another step of faith. They endure a little longer. Repeat.

Your faith pilgrimage has the same three elements.

Faith begins when you hear God saying to you, "I choose you. By my grace. You are my child." He bestows a new identity and a new destiny.

That brings you to a point of decision. Will you respond? Will you move toward him? Will you take the next step in whatever direction he sends you?

Then that initial response starts a lifelong process, a pilgrimage, as you grow into the person he saw when he chose you. Perseverance builds more perseverance.

But it starts with hearing him whisper his call.

> "You did not choose me, but I chose you..."
> (John 15:16 ESV)
>
> "He chose us in him before the foundation of the world..." (Ephesians 1:4 ESV)
>
> "God from the beginning chose you for salvation..."
> (2 Thessalonians 2:13 NKJV)

Will you respond with the next step in His direction?

36
what's
your call?

...to this you were called...

(1 Peter 3:9b)

**God's call is less about circumstances
than about character.
- Sherwood Carthen**

All through Hebrews 11 we've seen people called by God. So here's a question.

How do you know if God is calling you?

If you sense an urge to do something, is that God's call?
Are you disobedient if you do not follow that feeling?
And what if you don't sense God leading you to do anything?

I wrestled with this for years. I thought of God's call—God's will—as something fragile, easily missed and easily misunderstood. So I either followed every imagined "leading" about the tiniest details like precisely what color shirt to wear or what route to walk to school— or I was paralyzed by indecision, worried that if I somehow got God's will wrong, then I would be punished. So maybe it was better to do nothing at all. It drove me crazy.

As you can imagine, this had real-life repercussions.

For example, Laurie and I dated for four years. I knew her well. I loved her. We shared the same values. The same goals. The same faith. Yet I was hesitant to marry her for one reason: I did not feel "called". Practically every other Christian I knew claimed they felt a leading to marry that person (or take this job or move to that city). I was scanning my internal radar for blips of God's direction and drawing a big blank. What did it mean to "feel led" anyway? What if that feeling was just indigestion?

So I married Laurie because we were in love and we were compatible and for so many other reasons and more than three decades later our marriage is thriving and we enjoy one another and our beautiful growing family of three married children and three (soon to be five) grandchildren and have a rewarding ministry together. Sure glad I didn't wait for a "call".

And at pastor's conferences I would hear ministers talk about their "calling" to this or that church and usually I just sunk lower into my pew hoping not to be asked about my own call, petrified to reveal the truth: I never felt called to any church. Ever. When my current congregation asked me to be their pastor, I hemmed and hawed, waiting for The Call. Never got it. But it seemed a good match. So I went. Nearly 30 years later I am blessed to be part of a very joyful and fruitful church, to which I intend to remain faithful for as long as I can.

So I never really got the whole Call thing. Until I saw it in the Bible.

We are *all* called.

Yes, there are times God miraculously appears to a person like Abraham or Isaac or Gideon and calls them to a task. God can do whatever he wants to do. People can sense a call to a profession or ministry or task. But just as miraculously we have all been called through the Word of God, the Bible. Look what we are all called to:

> "Do not repay evil with evil or insult with insult. On the contrary, **repay evil with blessing**, because **to this you**

were called..." (1 Peter 3:9)

"As members of one body **you were called** to **peace**."
(Colossians 3:15)

"God reconciled us to himself through Christ and **gave us the ministry of reconciliation**." (2 Corinthians 5:18)

"You, my brothers and sisters, were **called to be free**. But do not use your freedom to indulge the flesh; rather, **serve one another humbly in love**." (Galatians 5:13)

"**Rejoice** always, **pray** continually, **give thanks** in all circumstances; for **this is God's will** for you in Christ Jesus." (1 Thessalonians 5:16-18)

"For **it is God's will** that by **doing good** you should silence the ignorant talk of foolish people."
(1 Peter 2:15)

"**It is God's will** that you should be sanctified: that you should avoid sexual immorality; that each of you should learn to **control your own body** in a way that is holy and honorable." (1 Thessalonians 4:3-4)

There it is. God's call. In black and white. In verses like these and others. God does not play games with you to see if you can read his mind. God is a great communicator. Will you obey his call?

This is important because when people focus too much on divining God's specific leading about personal details from urges and feelings, they can make odd missteps. I have lost track of how many times I have heard people validate the strangest decisions by claiming a "leading" from God.

I usually ask them questions:

Did you seek Scripture for guidance? "No."
Did you get advice from a godly person?
"No, just a feeling. I am following God's call like Abraham!"

Uh… why don't you pay closer attention to what God actually asked you to do in the Bible instead of anointing every impulse God's voice?

God called you to serve. To love. To be an ambassador. To develop Christ-like character.

When you are doing that, you are already in the will of God no matter your circumstances. If you are walking with God daily, growing in the fruit of the Spirit (Galatians 5:22-23), you don't have to worry about being out of the will of God because you missed some vague "call."

God's will for you is not fragile and easily missed.
God's will for you is clear and consistent.

Follow what you know to be his will, revealed for you in Scripture, and if you need more specific guidance, God is extremely capable of revealing that to you too. God will get you to where he wants you to be – even in spite of detours.

Think of these people we just met.

Joseph never got "called" to become Pharaoh's advisor. He just ended up there. Because God was working behind the scenes.

Isaac did get a clear call in a vision from God to move to Gerar and he deliberately ignored it—and God worked behind the scenes to maneuver him there anyway.

And you don't have to fear you missed God's call if your circumstances go sour. Abraham followed the specific instructions of God and had nothing to show for it for 24 long years before the blessing finally happened.

Don't worry about it. Just take the next step.

I eventually realized that so much of what I called "seeking God's will" was really about wanting to know the future. But fortune telling is not part of our faith. Daily obedience is.

Tomorrow is out of your control. This is the day the Lord has made. Rejoice in it. Obey in it.

This is what Abraham and the others did, however inconsistently. They responded to the revelation they had from God (for you and me that's the Bible) and trusted him for more specific direction should they need it later.

That is living faith forward.

37
faith hears the cheers

Therefore, since we are surrounded by such a great cloud of witnesses, let us throw off everything that hinders and the sin that so easily entangles, and let us run with perseverance the race marked out for us.

(Hebrews 12:1)

Faith remembers I am part of a team.

Think of the amazing people we've met in Hebrews 11.

We've seen faith in the life of old mom Sarah, old man Moses, bad girl Rahab, timid Gideon, teenage David, and many more. And now the writer to the Hebrews brings it all together in a great crescendo as he reveals something really amazing. It's the surprise ending I promised you.

All those people you've learned about, all those heroes... know about you. And are cheering you on like fans in a stadium cheering on their team.

How do I know? The Bible says so.

After zooming in tight on the faces of individuals throughout chapter 11, in the first few verses of Hebrews 12 there's a twist: the camera zooms out, way out, and reveals that all these famous faces are in the grandstands watching you run your race:

> "... we are surrounded by such a great cloud
> of witnesses..."

The words there are used in other ancient Greek writings for spectators at athletic events. I believe he really means what it sounds like he means: These people, in glory with Christ, are rooting for you.

I believe they are cheering with a wild enthusiasm born of personal investment, because, the way the author of Hebrews paints the picture, faith is not just a marathon race.

It's a marathon *relay* race. The baton has been passed from Abel to Enoch to Noah to Abraham, to all the patriarchs and prophets, to you!

I've mentioned that I was a long-distance runner in school, but don't get me wrong, I was no athlete. OK, I'll come right out and say it: I'm a klutz. Sometimes I think I'm one of the most uncoordinated people on the planet. The only sport I did in high school—the only sport I *could* do—was track, because it required an absolute minimum of hand-eye coordination. The coach would say: "Rene, listen carefully. When the man in the hat fires the gun, run! Run like the wind!

"Okay, coach!"

One day our mile relay team needed a runner for one of the four legs of their race because flu had swept through the group, and I was the only one available, much to the coach's chagrin (looking back, I realize a *lot* of people must have been sick for him to trust me with this). The mile relay was always the marquee event of our track meets, the last race of the day, by far the most exciting. Often teams would be tied going into the race, so the victorious school at the meet was determined by whoever won the relay. Each quarter-mile leg was typically run by the real celebrity runners, the true athletes at each school. Our flu-stricken team looked at me and got very worried.

My coach took me aside and wisely spent quite a long time telling me how to hold the baton, which had to be passed from one runner to the next. I have to say, that baton complicated the whole situation for me exponentially.

"Run while *holding* something? Do two things at once?!" I simply couldn't multi-task! I think the coach was afraid I'd just switch my focus throughout the race: "Run. Hold. Run. Hold. Run." I was terrified I'd drop it, or fling it wildly into the stands.

But that's not what made this race unforgettable. My single mom couldn't make it to many of my high school track meets due to her home daycare business. She had to work from morning to night, every day, just to make ends meet. That mile relay was the very first race of mine she ever saw. I had no idea she was there.

I was striding into the final stretch of my lap. My teammates in the stands were desperately screaming, "Go, Schlaepfer!" I was tired. It was an unfamiliar race. Other runners were catching up. I was super nervous about that baton. Then I heard Mom's high-pitched, Swiss-accented voice above all others, cheering me on like crazy: "Go, Schlaepfer!"

And I smiled and ran with a burst of fresh speed. We won the race and the meet and I still have nightmares about dropping batons.

There's nothing like a loved one's cheers to get you going. So if the thought of David and Moses cheering for you isn't enough, imagine who else is in that great cloud.

I think of Mom. My dad, Fred. My stepdad, Jet. Maybe you think of one of your parents, or a sibling, a child, or a friend. In heaven. Cheering you on like crazy.

Someone told me he suspected his many failures must be frustrating his heavenly fans. I see it a little differently. Ever watched a race where a runner falls, then gets back up again? The loudest, longest cheers of the day are usually for that athlete. Just for getting back in the game.

So shrug off the things that entangle you, all those petty sins and doubts. Listen to the cheers. For you. There's a new generation up ahead, waiting for that baton.

Run the race. One faith step at a time.

38
faith that
endures

...let us throw off everything that hinders and
the sin that so easily entangles...

(Hebrews 12:1b)

Faith plays the long game.

One Thanksgiving I ran the Silicon Valley Turkey Trot. Biggest in the nation. 28 thousand runners. The starting line is a party, with live bands, free food, and even a costume contest. I saw a runner dressed as a turkey, chased by his wife dressed as a chef. Indiana Jones was there. The winner was a giant spine, consisting of several runners from a chiropractor's office outfitted as vertebrae (I guess the whole team had to run single-file or they'd be out of alignment).

How many of these costumes do you think you see at the finish line? Not many! At the end of my race there was not a costume runner in sight.

My point? To quote John Ortberg,

> "The start of a race is enjoyable. It is easy.
> Finishing is hard work."

This applies to all of life. Finishing *anything* is harder than starting. Living faith forward is not a sprint. It's a marathon. So the author of Hebrews gives a key to endurance. Any distance runner would agree:

Run light.

That costume is not doing you any favors.

> "…let us throw off everything that hinders and the sin that so easily entangles…" Hebrews 12:1b

You don't run a marathon with a backpack.

Most Christians carry a lot of extra pounds. Regrets. Worries. Distractions. One of the most common weights I see: Bitterness. That's why later in this same chapter the author warns against the "bitter root that grows up to cause trouble." (Hebrews 12:15)

So get rid of the excess baggage.

> "… and the sin which so easily entangles…"
> (Hebrews 12:1b)

In the original Greek, the writer uses a definite article. "*The* sin." He seems to be referring to the specific sin that is likely to trip you up. What is it for *you*? It's got to go. Even if everyone else is doing it.

Some of you are thinking, "Well, it's too late for me. I've already blown it. I have tripped up so many times in the race." Wrong! Your race is not over. So you tripped and fell. What are you going to do from here on? Today? The next step?

Look at the rest of verse one:

> "…and let us run with perseverance the race marked out for us." Heb.12:1c (NIV)

Not "let us run with regret the race we wished we had run."

Don't look back. Not even at your failures. Keep living faith *forward*.

39
faith stays
focused

Let us fix our eyes on Jesus, the author and
perfecter of our faith...

(Hebrews 12:2a)

Faith fights distractions with focus.

Now I will tell you something very personal as we reach the end of this book together. Several years ago, I was extremely discouraged in my ministry. Even as I preached one Sunday I was thinking of quitting. Wondering who else I could work for.

After that church service, an elderly man came up to me. Fred Moody. I hadn't seen Fred in decades, since he was my fourth-grade Sunday School teacher. Fred says, "Rene, I don't know why, but I feel I need to tell you this. I was with your dad when he died. I was right next to him."

I was riveted. I was only four when dad died and I had never spoken to someone who was there.

"During those last hours," Fred said, "Your father's favorite song brought him so much comfort." And right then and there, Fred closed his eyes and began to sing it for me. All the noise of the post-church scene faded as I listened to him sing these words:

> Turn your eyes upon Jesus.
> Look full in his wonderful face.
> And the things of earth
> Will grow strangely dim
> In the light of his glory and grace.

Since that moment I have often thought of my dad in that great cloud of witnesses, yelling from the stands,

"Turn your eyes on Jesus, son! Turn your eyes on Jesus."

After his stunning list of faith heroes, the author of Hebrews is not quite done. He saved the best for last. The other heroes are inspiring. But the single most motivating thing you can do as a Christian? Focus on **Jesus**.

Earlier in Hebrews the author has argued argued that Jesus is their best bet. Jesus is stronger, holier, steadier, greater, wiser than any prophet or angel. He's more beautiful, he's more trustworthy, he's blameless, pure, exalted. He's our ultimate hope. Even when we feel like drifting away, even when everything else disappoints, even when there are a million things about life and church that are annoying and confusing, he's the One worth focusing on.

But that's not easy. The race is filled with distractions. From every corner on the course, alarms blare and temptations allure. We get distracted by pop culture, politics, problems, pressures, people. Our message to a watching world gets confused as they see us veer off track, changing direction constantly.

The first Christians had all sorts of distractions and disagreements too, deeply held differences threatening to blow up the early church. So the author of Hebrews tells them to focus.

We need to hear this. In our church there are a huge variety of opinions. And that's as it should be. We have every kind of person and personality. We have Christians at every level of maturity. People disagree about music style, church style, movies, drinking, diet, entertainment, politics, and much more. But we still have one thing in common: Our faith in Christ.

So let's make every effort to focus on the Lord we love.
Because that's where the joy is.

> "Let us fix our eyes on Jesus, the author and perfecter
> of our faith, who for the joy set before him endured the
> cross, scorning its shame, and sat down at the right
> hand of the throne of God." (Hebrews 12:2)

That joy is before you too. The Bible says one day in heaven
we will be with Jesus as a pure and spotless bride.
That means all the sin,
All the tears,
All the disease,
All the division,
All the distraction,
All the grief and pain and sorrow,
All gone, as we live together
In resurrected perfection.

That is the finish line. That is the goal. That is what
distinguishes Hebrews 11 from a self-improvement message.
The big idea is not **try harder**. It's **trust Jesus**.

When you turn your eyes on Jesus, when you trust his
character even when you have questions, then the things
that worry you and distract you and tempt you here really will
grow dim in the light of his glory and his grace.

Keep it simple. Get back on track. Focus on Christ. That is
what strengthens the church. That is what changes the world.

That is living faith forward.

40
faith forward

Let us hold firmly to the
faith we profess.

(Hebrews 4:14)

Faith keeps the main thing the main thing.

Today I was talking to a friend who is a scientist and an atheist. One of his brothers is a strong Christian who was visiting from out of town with his family. I asked how it went.

"Oh, you know, I always get into trouble with them," he said.

"Trouble?"

"Yeah, they're always on me about something. Like swearing. And they always talk about Christianity, all the time."

"Really? Like, what do they talk about?"

"You know, Christianity: What they hate about politicians. What they hate about culture. What they hate about TV. What they hate about the country. Faith stuff."

"Uh... do they ever say anything about... Jesus?"

He thought for a while. "Nope."

I wanted to cry.

We are not so much losing faith as diluting faith. We are adding so much to Jesus that you can hardly see him anymore. Like hoarders crowding a house with all their junk, we just can't seem to resist any distraction.

The author of Hebrews is seeing the same exact problem. The original readers are allowing themselves to be distracted by all sorts of debates and teachings. They are fighting among themselves about what "true" Christians should or should not be doing. Of course they are finding their faith grow cold. Their focus is not on faith anymore. So the author keeps pulling them back to the main thing:

> "We must pay more careful attention to what we have heard, so that we do not **drift away**." (Hebrews 2:1)

> "...**fix your thoughts on Jesus**." (Hebrews 3:1)

> "Let us **hold firmly** to the faith we profess." (Hebrews 4:1b)

> "Let us **hold unswervingly** to the hope we profess..." (Hebrews 10:23)

> "Let us **fix our eyes** on Jesus..." (Hebrews 12:2)

> "**Do not be carried away** by all kinds of strange teachings." (Hebrews 13:9)

How many ways can the writer say, "Focus, people!?"

I've been using the phrase *faith forward* as a summary of what Hebrews 11 is all about. Here's what I mean: I hear the phrase "fruit forward" sometimes applied to wine. It means wine that tastes like, well, fruit. It's a good thing for wines to have a complex flavor profile. I've heard real wine lovers describe flavors of mushrooms, leather, earth, tea, peppercorns, cigar box, forest floor, and even "wet dog" (no thanks).

But too many Christians have developed what you could call an overly complex flavor profile. We have complicated a great taste with aromas of politics, culture wars, legalism, and debates over every issue known to humanity. Jesus gets overpowered by wet dog and mushroom.

Let's be Christians that taste like Christ. Faith forward.

I also like *"faith forward"* because it connotes *momentum*.
As we've seen, faith is not just words. It's action.
Faith moves. Faith lives.
Faith is going somewhere, answering God's call.

Living faith forward means you lead with what's most important and follow with what's less important. It means the first thing people say about you is not "I'm always in trouble with them" but "I always know I'm loved by them." It means if anyone ever says you're "always talking about your faith" it's because you're talking about loving God and loving others. It means if people suspect you might be a Christian it's because you actually live like Christ. It means your faith is not just a noun, it's a verb. It means you don't get secondary and tertiary issues confused with primary issues.

Living faith forward is not about compromising anything. It's about prioritizing the important things.

We have been distracted and discouraged for too long.
We have been politics-forward, culture-forward, fear-forward, trend-forward, division-forward, issue-forward, rules-forward, opinion-forward, family-forward, fashion-forward, celebrity-forward.

Let's get focused. Let's make progress.

Let's live faith forward.

now what?

What's the next step in the race of faith for you?

Some of you are just thinking about starting the race.

We've been studying faith for several weeks and maybe you're still considering it. Enter the race today. I urge you to pray a simple prayer of surrender to Christ. He is calling. Step out in faith. It is so worth it.

Maybe you are in the first hundred yards. You just started.

Get in a training routine. Start daily meditations, memorizing Bible verses, staying in regular weekly fellowship. Enduring is about small steps, taken consistently, to get you to your goal. So initiate simple, daily, steady faith habits.

Maybe you're in the "grind it out" phase of the race, somewhere in the lonely middle miles, running in the rain and in the dark, overwhelmed with life.

You know what helps more than anything in that phase? Finding running partners. So your next step is: Reach out. Get connected. Call your church and get a faith mentor. Join a small group. Make a phone call to a friend you haven't spoken to in years.

Maybe you're in the sprint toward the end. You're gassed,

exhausted, but the goal's in sight.

Don't give up. Keep your eyes on Christ. Listen to the cheers. And if you can't hear the cheers, contact your church. You can get put on the prayer list and the whole prayer team will be cheering you on and praying for you.

My prayer for you: That you may be able to say what Paul said at the end of his life:

> "I have finished the race, I have kept the faith."
> (2 Timothy 4:7)

That is possible. Just take the next step.

small group discussion guides

small group discussion guide week 1

what does faith think like?

PRAYER

Ask God to bless your time together. Ask Him to help you have open minds and hearts to His leading.

OPENER

Introduce yourselves and answer one or both of the following questions:

We'll be looking at many stories of biblical heroes in this series. **What is your favorite movie or book about a hero?** Why?

We'll be looking at how to build up faith in this series. **What is one faith-building habit you started in the last few months?** How has it helped you?

ORIENTATION

Have someone read Hebrews 11:1-6 out loud.

VIDEO

Watch this week's video lesson together.

> "Without faith it is impossible to please God, because anyone who comes to Him must believe **He exists** and that **He rewards** those who earnestly seek Him." (Hebrews 11:6)

At its most basic, faith involves choosing to trust that

God is __real__

God is __good__

Note: The following is not a complete *definition* of faith. This is a partial *description* of faith. These are a few of the many themes of Hebrews 11.

Faith involves:

1. <u>Believing</u> when I don't see it.

   "Now faith is being sure of what we hope for and **certain of what we do not see**." (Hebrews 11:1)

2. <u>Obeying</u> when I don't understand it.

   "It was faith that made Abraham obey when God called him and go out to a country God had promised to him. He left his own country **without knowing where he was going**." (Hebrews 11:8 GN)

3. <u>Trusting God</u> if I don't get it.

   "All these people were still living by faith when they died. **They did not receive the things promised**; they only saw them and welcomed them from a distance, admitting that they were foreigners and strangers on earth." (Hebrews 11:12)

   "They were all commended for their faith yet **none of them received** what had been promised. **God had planned something better**..."
   (Hebrews 11:39-40)

DISCUSSION

1. Which of the three aspects of faith described in the video is easiest for you? Which is the biggest challenge?

2. Give an example from your life when you practiced one of these aspects of faith.

3. Share from your life where you are currently struggling to apply one of these aspects of faith.

4. According to Hebrews 11:6, what two things must we believe to have faith? What kind of person do you think that produces?

5. How is biblical faith different than positive, wishful, or magical thinking?

6. Rene writes in the book about how the original readers of Hebrews had been strong through struggles, but now felt tired and beaten up. Do you relate? How do you hope this study on faith can help?

LIVING FAITH FORWARD

Be on the lookout for ways God is teaching you about faith this week. Come prepared to share next week.

PRAYER

Share prayer requests and close your time together as a group with prayer.

small group discussion guide week 2

what does faith act like?

PRAYER

Ask God to bless your time together. Ask Him to help you have open minds and hearts to His leading.

OPENER

Are you naturally a risk-taker or risk-avoider? What challenges in life tend to scare you?

Did God teach you something about faith this week?

ORIENTATION

Have someone read Hebrews 11:8-16 out loud. How did Abraham and Sarah demonstrate their faith in God?

VIDEO

Watch this week's video lesson together.

Faith is not the greatest risk.
The greatest risk is _____ .
(See Jesus' parable in Matthew 25:24-27)

> "By faith Abraham, when called to go to a place he would later receive as his inheritance, obeyed and went, even though he did not know where he was going."
> (Hebrews 11:8)

This is what faith acts like:

1. Faith is _____ when God

_____ .

2. Faith is _____ when God

_____ .

Why am I afraid of failure?
Do I live by my performance or on the basis of Christ's power?
Have I gotten this far on my efforts or by the grace of God?
What will I lose through failure anyway?
I still have God's love, His kindness,
And if I do fail here, he will only use it to prepare me for something greater
My worthiness is not based on my success.
Jesus is my security.
And as a result I don't have to worry about failure here.
I'm free from fear.

-Tim Keller

DISCUSSION

1. Do you tend to demonstrate "adventurous faith," or do you tend to stay conservative with your risks?

2. Has there ever been a time in your life when you moved out in faith? What happened?

3. Biblically speaking, fear and faith are not a product of temperament. They are controllable responses. What have you found to be helpful in building up your courage in faith?

4. What advice would you give others fearful of moving out in faith?

5. The Bible talks a lot about risk-taking in faith, yet it also talks a lot about wisdom ("The wise man built his house upon a rock," said Jesus). So both stability and mobility are part of a life of faith. If you have security in Christ, you can risk mobility for Christ. How does this work out in practical ways in real life?

LIVING FAITH FORWARD

What potentially scary new place is God calling you to go in faith-- someplace out of your comfort zone? To renew a broken friendship? To forgive someone who has hurt you? To reach out in love to a neighbor? Share a commitment with your group about how you will live "faith forward" this week.

One way we'll ask you to move out in faith during this series: Choosing a way for you or your group to serve those in need. You may choose to participate sacrificially in a food drive, or in a service project, or by adopting someone in your neighborhood who needs help. Begin now to pray and dream about this as a group.

PRAYER

Share prayer requests and close your time together as a group with prayer.

small group discussion guide week 3

**getting past the
faith-killing excuses**

PRAYER

Ask God to bless your time together. Ask Him to help you have open minds and hearts to His leading.

OPENER

Do you tend to be a procrastinator or do you get your work done fast?

How has this study of faith has impacted your life so far? Are there any concepts from the sermons or devotionals that have been particularly impactful?

ORIENTATION

Have group members read Hebrews 11:24-27 and Exodus 3:1-11 out loud.

VIDEO

Watch this week's lesson together.

Getting Past 4 Faith-Killing Excuses:
(Read along by opening your Bible to Exodus 3 and 4)

Excuse #1: _____
(Exodus 3:11)

    God's answer: _____
    (Exodus 3:12; Matt. 28:20)

Excuse #2: _____
(Exodus 3:13)

God's answer: _____
(Exodus 3:14-16; 1 Jn 1:3)

Excuse #3: _____
(Exodus 4:1)

God's answer: _____
(Exodus 4:2-9; Acts 1:8)

Excuse #4: _____
(Exodus 4:10)

God's answer: _____
(Exodus 4:11,14; Lk 12:11-12)

Nothing ever happens to people who always say ____ .

DISCUSSION

1. Which of Moses' excuses do you identity with, or tend to use most often?

2. Which of God's answers do you most need to hear right now to help build your faith? Why?

3. Share a time in your life when you were afraid to move out in faith, made excuses, but moved ahead anyway. What happened? What did God teach you through that time?

4. How have you seen God's faithfulness in the last few weeks?

LIVING FAITH FORWARD

What is one way you will move ahead in faith this week that you have been putting off with excuses? Forgiving someone? Volunteering? Reaching out to a neighbor? Share your commitment with the group and ask for prayer.

How will you or your group put your faith into action to serve those in need? You may choose to participate sacrificially in a food drive, or in a service project, by "adopting" someone in your neighborhood who needs help, or maybe you have another idea. Discuss some ideas with your group.

PRAYER

Share prayer requests and close your time together as a group with prayer.

small group discussion guide week 4

faith when you hit a wall

PRAYER

Ask God to bless your time together. Ask Him to help you have open minds and hearts to His leading.

OPENER

Last week we agreed to move ahead in faith in some area where you were making excuses. What did you do? What happened?

Today we are talking about faith when you "hit a wall." Who have you known personally who persevered well through troubled times? What seemed to be their secret?

ORIENTATION

Have someone read Joshua 6:1-16 out loud.

VIDEO

Watch this week's lesson together.

> "By faith the walls of Jericho fell, after the army had marched around them for seven days." (Hebrews 11:30)

Three keys to faith when facing a wall:

1. Trust that God's ___victory is certain___ (even when it seems ___evil is winning___)

> "And those he predestined, he also called; those he called, he also justified; those he justified, he also glorified." (Romans 8:30)

2. Trust that God's _instruction is wise_ (even when it seems _ridiculous_)

3. Trust that God's _timing is perfect_ (even when it seems _to take forever_)

Just because _____ isn't _____
Doesn't mean _____ isn't _____

Obedience is my responsibility
Outcome is God's responsibility

> "Let us not become weary in doing good, for at the proper time we will reap a harvest if we do not give up." (Galatians 6:9)

DISCUSSION

1. In what kinds of circumstances do you find it most difficult to persevere and stay positive: sudden large disasters, constant low-grade stresses, persistent small annoyances, or something else?

2. Have you ever hit a wall in your own life and still persevered? What happened and what did you find helpful?

3. Which of the three keys to faith from the video is easiest for you? Which is most difficult?

4. Where do you feel you are "hitting a wall" right now?

5. Where does Joshua's faith story resonate with you in terms of the challenges you are facing right now?

LIVING FAITH FORWARD

Share prayer requests about where you need faith to "not stop on six" in your life right now. Come prepared to share next week about how that's going.

How will you or your group put your faith into action to serve those in need? You may choose to participate sacrificially in a food drive, or in a service project, by "adopting" someone in your neighborhood who needs help, or maybe you have another idea. Discuss some ideas with your group.

PRAYER

Share prayer requests and close your time together as a group with prayer.

small group discussion guide week 5

faith when you feel inadequate

PRAYER

Ask God to bless your time together. Ask Him to help you have open minds and hearts to His leading.

OPENER

Last week we shared where you need to not "stop on six"—to persevere in faith. How did that go for you this past week?

This week we will see how God encourages someone who felt weak. Do you tend to dwell on your own successes or your failures?

ORIENTATION

Have someone read Hebrews 11:32-34 and Judges 6:11-16 out loud.

VIDEO

Watch this week's lesson together.

> "When the angel of the Lord appeared to Gideon, he said, "The Lord is with you, mighty warrior."
> (Judges 6:12)
>
> "The Lord is with you, mighty man of valor!" (NKJV)
>
> "The Lord is with you, you mighty man of fearless courage!" (Amplified)

God does not see you for what you _____.

God sees you for what you _____.

We see ourselves in terms of yesterday and today.
God sees us in terms of tomorrow and forever.

1. Are you _____ to what God is saying to you…
   about you?

> "He chose us in him before the creation of the world to
> be holy and blameless in his sight." (Ephesians 1:4)

> "See what great love the Father has lavished on us, that
> we should be called children of God! And that is what we
> are!" (1 John 3:1a)

> "You are a chosen people, a royal priesthood, a holy
> nation, God's special possession, that you may declare
> the praises of him who called you out of darkness into
> his wonderful light." (1 Peter 2:9)

2. Are you _____ what God is saying to others…
   about them?

> "By our speech we can ruin the world, turn harmony to
> chaos, throw mud on a reputation, send the whole world
> up in smoke and go up in smoke with it, smoke right
> from the pit of hell." (James 3:5, The Message)

> "Do not let any unwholesome talk come out of your
> mouths, but only what is helpful for building others up
> according to their needs, that it may benefit those who
> listen." (Ephesians 4:29 NIV)

DISCUSSION

1. Do you tend to picture God being critical of you or encouraging you? Why do you think you have this picture of God? Has this changed over the years for you?

2. When you read the verses under point 1 about how God sees you in Christ, do you drink it all in eagerly—or do you resist it a little? Why?

3. Rene told the story of his aunt Pia speaking words of faith to him when he was a child. Has anyone spoken words of faith to you that encouraged you in the past? A parent? Coach? Teacher? Friend? Pastor?

4. Do you tend to be critical or encouraging? Has this changed over the years?

MOVING FORWARD

Share with the group a specific person to whom you will be "Gideon's angel" to this week. Come prepare to share what happened when you meet next week.

Has your group chosen a big "faith forward" act of kindness yet? Discuss your plans with each other. Are you feeling any hesitation? Why? How can these lessons in faith help you?

PRAYER

Share prayer requests and close your time together as a group with prayer.

small group discussion guide week 6

faith when facing giants

OPENER

Last week we talked about being the voice of "Gideon's angel" to a specific person. Did you do that? What happened?

Today we will see an underdog triumph against a giant. What is one of your favorite "underdog" stories in sports, movies, or books?

ORIENTATION

Have someone read 1 Samuel 17:1-50. This is a longer passage than I normally ask you to read, but it is a great story. Don't worry about pronouncing the names correctly, just follow the exciting plot!

VIDEO

Watch this week's lesson together.

1. Refuse to see only _____ (1 Samuel 17:26)

2. Reframe _____ (1 Samuel 17:37)

3. Remember _____ (1 Samuel 17:45,47)

4. Run _____ (1 Samuel 17:48)

DISCUSSION

1. What "giant" are you facing? In what ways does it challenge your faith?

2. Which of the four points is hardest for you? Which is easiest?

3. Do you tend to spend more time thinking about the Goliath who taunts you—or the God who strengthens you? How can you increase your God-thoughts and decrease your Goliath-thoughts?

4. Here's a question that will take real transparency, so please only share if you feel comfortable. David found courage by reframing past trauma—remembering how the Lord had helped him in the past with lions or bears. What "lion or bear" have you confronted in the past—a giant difficulty or problem—that the Lord has helped you with? How have you reframed that past trauma in a way that gives you faith to face the future?

LIVING FAITH FORWARD

What giant are you facing right now that you'd like the group to pray about?

Who do you know facing a giant right now? How could you or your group encourage them?

What will you be doing for your "faith in action" project? If you haven't done it yet, discuss it with your group.

PRAYER

Share prayer requests and close your time together as a group with prayer.

small group discussion guide week 7

finishing the race of faith

OPENER

When you were a kid on a road trip, did you ever feel like the trip was taking forever? Where were you going? Did you parents do anything that helped?

Describe which of these it feels like in your life right now, and why:

> Thinking of starting
> The first mile!
> Whoops, I just tripped.
> The lonely middle miles
> The Wall
> Seeing the finish line

ORIENTATION

Read Hebrews 11:32-12:3

VIDEO

Watch this week's lesson together.

How can runners finish strong in the marathon of faith? (Hebrews 12:1,2)

1. Run _____

> "Therefore, since we are surrounded by such a great cloud of witnesses…"

2. Run _____

> "…let us throw off everything that hinders and the sin that so easily entangles."

3. Run _____

   "And let us run with perseverance the race marked out for us…"

4. Run _____

   "…fixing our eyes on Jesus, the pioneer and perfecter of faith. For the joy set before him he endured the cross, scorning its shame, and sat down at the right hand of the throne of God."

DISCUSSION

1. In this week's section of Hebrews, the writer makes one thing clear: Faith does not guarantee a life of ease. The people he records had just about everything fall apart, mostly because they were persecuted for their faith. What are the dangers of seeing faith as a way to a trouble-free life?

2. Who have you known who seemed particularly successful at keeping the faith in troubled times? What seemed to be their secret?

3. Rene mentioned "running light." What distraction or sin do you need to get rid of in order to strengthen your faith?

4. "Run steady" was one of the points. Is it difficult for you to pace yourself—Do you tend to be a "workaholic for Jesus"? How can you work rest and recuperation into your own walk of faith—what have you specifically found helpful?

5. "Run focused" was another point. What do you think can be distractions today from the beauty and example of Jesus? What distracts you? How can you focus on Jesus in a more effective way by eliminating distractions?

LIVING FAITH FORWARD

How will you apply one of these specific points to your life this week?

PRAYER

Share with your Small Group the tough times you are going through for which you would like prayer.

small group discussion guide week 8

faith and gratitude

There's no video discussion starter for this week. This is the week to celebrate what God has done through this study in your life, and to pray for further growth!

OPENER

What food do you love most at Thanksgiving?

What are you thankful for in your life?

ORIENTATION

Go around the group and read Psalm 107. This is almost like another version of Hebrews 11. The courage of these people was failing. But they gave thanks to the Lord for his unfailing love and his deeds for all people, and their faith was strengthened.

DISCUSSION

1. How do you think gratitude strengthens faith?

2. What character in Hebrews 11 did you relate to most?

3. Look over this review of our Hebrews 11 series:

In week 1 we talked about how faith thinks: Believing God is real, God is good, and God rewards—even when I cannot see Him working. Faith is entrustment.

In week 2 we talked about how faith acts: Taking the first step even when I don't see the whole staircase.

In week 3 we talked about getting past faith-killing excuses. I have God's presence and power, and I have a testimony and a team. I am not alone.

Week 4 was about trusting when I hit a wall, like Joshua. Just because progress isn't happening doesn't mean God isn't working. Obedience is my responsibility. Outcome is God's responsibility.

In week 5 God's angel called Gideon, hiding in a hole, a "mighty man of valor." I asked, "Am I listening to what God is saying?" and "Am I speaking what God is saying?"

Week 6 was about facing giants like David did: Seeing the rewards, reframing past trauma, remembering God's strength, and running to battle.

In week 7 we looked at finishing the marathon. Long distance races are about running light (eliminating distraction), running steady (pacing myself), and running focused (on Jesus).

What point or principle in this series really jumped out at you?

4. What is your next step of faith?

PRAYER

Take some time to specifically pray for one another and the faith challenges you are facing. Pray also for our county, country, and the world and the challenges we are facing.

Pray that followers of Jesus would be beacons of God's light where hope grows dim. May we be agents of faith to a despairing world!

acknowledg-ments

I make no claims to originality in this book and have tried to give credit by name when I know the source of a quote or idea. However! I freely acknowledge that I tend to remember little turns of phrase I find clever (while somehow also forgetting the names of people I've known for decades). Over the years I have also written tons of handwritten notes on sermons which unfortunately look like scribbled phrases with many underlines and stars and exclamation marks and absolutely no indication whether I thought this line up or heard it from someone else. I am resolving to change! In the meantime please assume every cool line in this book was thought up by someone else.

I found particularly helpful David Tieche's new book *Abraham: A Field Guide to Loving God*, Ray Stedman's commentary on Hebrews, Patrick Gray and Amy Peeler's scholarly work on Hebrews, Saddleback Church's sermon series on Hebrews, the *New International Commentary on the New Testament: The Epistle of Hebrews* by Gareth Lee Cockerill, and Paul David Tripp's *40 Days of Faith*.

I also adapted a couple daily readings from my own previous books *Chasing David* and *God Is*.

end-notes

Chapter 5

"an uncanny optimism…" from Blaine Smith, *The Optimism Factor*, Chapter 2

"Faith does not just mean…" from Paul David Tripp, *40 Days of Faith*, p. 9

Chapter 6

Reports on health benefits of church attendance can be found here:

https://www.washingtonpost.com/news/acts-of-faith/wp/2016/05/16/another-possible-benefit-of-going-to-worship-services-a-33-percent-chance-of-living-longer/

https://www.healthstatus.com/health_blog/wellness/the-top-health-benefits-of-church-attendance/

"It confounds my ideological beliefs…" from Matthew Parris, "As an atheist, I truly believe Africa needs God," The Times of London, December 27, 2008, https://www.thetimes.co.uk/

Chapter 7

"The discovery recently…" from Stephen Hawking, *The Grand Design*, p. 162

"The multi-verse theory…" from Paul Davies, "Taking Science on Faith", *New York Times*, November 24, 2007

"The more I examine…" from Freeman Dyson, *Scientific American*, 224, 1971, p 50

"the expression of the purposive design…" from John Polkinghorne, *Science and Theology*, p. 75.

Chapter 9

"If you wish to truly…" from Carl Sagan, *Cosmos* TV series, "Lives of the Stars" episode

Chapter 10

"Sacrifice is acceptable…" from F. F. Bruce, *The Epistle to the Hebrews*, p. 281

Chapter 12

Dashrath Manjhi's story from Wikipedia and https://www.indiatoday.in/education-today/gk-current-affairs/story/dashrath-manjhi-282520-2015-07-15

Chapter 13
Richard Wiseman's research on luck is recounted in his book *The Luck Factor* (Miramax Books, 2003).

Chapter 15
"It's like in the great stories…" Quoted in Sylvie Magerstaedt, *Philosophy, Myth, and Epic Cinema*, p. 114

"…smelled a sweet fragrance…" from J.R.R. Tolkien, *The Return of the King*, p. 339

Chapter 16
"More than any other moment…" from David Tieche, *Abraham: A Field Guide to Loving God*

Chapter 19
"some of the smartest…" and "In the end, we will measure…" from Clayton M. Christensen, "How Will You Measure Your Life?" *Harvard Business Review Classics*, 2017

Gallup World Poll data from research at https://www.gallup.com/analytics/349487/gallup-global-happiness-center.aspx

Chapter 21
"It is not the quality…" from Tim Keller tweet, March 13, 2019, https://twitter.com/dailykeller/status/1105824185237020673

Chapter 24
"Don't stop on six!" and idea about God speaking in past tense about future events from Steven Furtick, "Don't Stop on Six", sermon preached at Elevation Church, Nov. 4, 2013, https://www.youtube.com/watch?v=B24VMvTN9fk

Chapter 25
Thanks to Adrian Moreno for some great material about Rahab from a sermon he preached at Twin Lakes Church as part of our "Promised Land Living" series

Chapter 28
"…A surprising and welcome discovery…" from Max Lucado, *Begin Again*, p. 25

Chapter 29
"Grace calls out…" from Brennan Manning, *The Ragamuffin Gospel*, p. 14

Chapter 30
"Tania Luna, psychologist and author…" from *The Power of Optimism*, Meredith Publishing, 2021, p. 79

Chapter 34
Marla Runyan story and quotes from Debra Michals, "Marla Runyan," *National Women's History Museum* www.womenshistory.org/education-resources/biographies/marla-runyan and David Jeremiah, *Overcomers*, p. 106

Chapter 38
"The start of a race…" from John Ortberg, *The Life You've Always Wanted*, p. 209